Published by
Beyond Words Publishing, Inc.
20827 NW Cornell Road, Suite 500
Hillsboro, Oregon 97124
503-531-8700/1-800-284-9673

The information contained in this book is intended to be educational and not for diagnosis, prescription, or treatment of mental and/or physical health disorders, whatsoever. This information should not replace competent medical and/or psychological care. The authors and publisher are in no way liable for any use or misuse of the information.

ISBN: 1-58270-045-1

Authors: Laura Carlsmith, Barbara Mann, Michelle Roehm McCann, and Emily Strelow
Design: Andrea L. Boven / Boven Design Studio, Inc.
Proofreader: Susan Beal

Every effort has been made to contact the copyright owners of the photographs in this book. If the copyright holder of a photograph in this book has not heard from us, please contact Beyond Words Publishing. The publisher gratefully acknowledges and thanks the following for generous assistance and permission to use photos:

Jonny Lang: Photgraph by Kim Schles, Courtesy of Vector Management
David Leung: Courtesy of California Jump$tart and ExactImage.com
Iqbal Masih: Courtesy of The Reebok Human Rights Program

"On Growing Up" Copyright ©2001 by Mattie J.T. Stepanek

Printed in the United States of America
Distributed to the book trade by Publishers Group West

Library of Congress Cataloging-in-Publication Data

Boys who rocked the world : from King Tut to Tiger Woods / written by the editors of Beyond Words Publishing ; illustrated by Lar DeSouza.
p. cm.
ISBN 1-58270-045-1 (softcover)
  [1. Boys—Biography—Juvenile literature. 2. Heroes— Biography—Juvenile literature. 1. Boys. 2. Heroes.] I. DeSouza, Lar, ill. II. Beyond Words Publishing.
CT107 .B65 2001
920.02—dc21   2001028424

The corporate mission of Beyond Words Publishing, Inc:
Inspire to Integrity

BOYS WHO ROCKED THE WORLD

From King Tut to Tiger Woods

Written by the Editors of Beyond Words Publishing
Illustrated by Lar DeSouza

BEYOND
WORDS
Publishing
I N C

On Growing Up

We are growing up.

We are many colors of skin.

We are many languages.

We are many ages and sizes.

We are many countries…

But we are one earth.

We each have one heart.

We each have one life.

We are growing up, together,

So we must live as one family.

—MATTIE J.T. STEPANEK

Table of Contents

Boys Who Are Rocking the World Right Now!

King Tutankhamun

1347 BC - 1329 BC ✚ Pharaoh ✚ Egypt

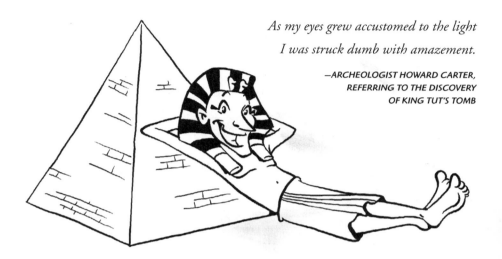

*As my eyes grew accustomed to the light
I was struck dumb with amazement.*

—ARCHEOLOGIST HOWARD CARTER,
REFERRING TO THE DISCOVERY
OF KING TUT'S TOMB

Ten-year-old Tutankhamun nervously approached the great Karnak Temple. The last in a long line of rulers, young Tut was to be crowned pharaoh of Egypt. It was now his job to oversee the largest empire in the world, which stretched from Africa to Asia. *Will I be remembered as a great leader, too?* he wondered as he walked past the great monuments and statues of the pharaohs who ruled before him. The cheers from the crowd at the temple grew to a deafening roar as the boy entered. Would the boy pharaoh bring prosperity back to Egypt? He was their last hope.

Several priests poured sacred water from golden urns over Tut. Then they placed the magnificent three crowns of Egypt on his head. There was the tall, white crown of Lower Egypt, then the red crown of Upper Egypt, and finally the *Kepresh*, a blue crown representing Egypt's vast armies. Thousands of Egyptians looked on in hushed silence as the priests balanced the triple crown on Tut's small head.

Pharaoh means "one who resides in the palace." ❖

Even though his reign was brief—only nine years—Tut's dream to be remembered came true. Though he ruled over 3,000 years ago, he is now the most well-known of all the Egyptian pharaohs. As ruler, he helped return a crumbling empire to its former prosperity and stability. His tomb, filled with an immense wealth of gold and priceless artifacts—as well as a mysterious curse—has only helped solidify young Tut's legend.

King Tut was born in 1347 BC in Egypt's rich, green Nile valley. His name, Tutankhamun, meant "strong bull," which suited Tut well. As a young man, he was praised for his strength and skills as a hunter of ostriches, peacocks, ibexes, gazelles and wild hippos. His father was the Pharaoh Akhenaten, who was not well-liked by Egyptians since he had defied the traditional religion, which had many gods, and singled out one god as worthy of worship. Akhenaten had also moved the capitol from Thebes to Amarna, further angering his people.

Growing up in Amarna, young Tut was a bit of a slacker. His older brother Smenkare was next in line to be pharaoh, so not much was expected of Tut. When he wasn't learning to read or write Egyptian hiero-glyphs (pictures that represent words), Tut did what most kids do today: he goofed off. He hunted and raced around in chariots, played *Senet*, his favorite board game, and swam in the Nile with his siblings.

In his tomb, Tut was buried with over 140 pieces of jewelry, including fifteen rings, thirteen bracelets, many amulets, and a crown made of pure gold. He also had 93 pairs of shoes and 415 statues of servants to serve him in the afterlife. ❖

When Tut was seven years old, he received the shock of his life. Smenkare got very sick and died. Suddenly, Tut was destined to inherit all his father's duties as pharaoh of Egypt. No more slacking—it was time to cram! Tut's lessons got a lot harder as he prepared for his new role. Good thing he crammed…just two years later his father died. Only nine years old, Tut was now the ruler of the Egyptian empire and had the huge responsibility of unifying Egypt after his father's rocky reign.

Tut decided to bring back the traditional religion his father had outlawed and returned the capital to Thebes. When the young pharaoh moved back to the capital, a coronation ceremony was arranged so that all of Egypt could be introduced to their new boy king. Once crowned, Tut quickly ordered the rebuilding of the old temples that had fallen into disrepair during his father's reign. With the guidance of priests, he performed ceremonies to improve the harvest (most people in Egypt made their living from farming). Tut was also in charge of Egypt's gigantic army, and with the help of his military advisors, he won several battles.

By age fifteen, Tut was growing into a strong and trustworthy leader. He brought stability back to Lower and Upper Egypt, and comfort to people who honored the traditional religion. Tut was also proving to be a skilled negotiator, helping to solidify relations between Egypt's neighbors, Assyria and Babylonia. Egypt, which had experienced dark days during Akhenaten's reign, was making a comeback. Crops along the Nile were bountiful and Egypt's many storehouses overflowed.

> In ancient Egypt, men and women both wore black eye make-up made of black lead ore. The make-up was considered stylish but also helped protect the Egyptians from eye infections and the harsh, desert sun. ❖

But King Tut's reign ended almost as quickly as it began. At the age of eighteen, King Tutankhamun suddenly died. No one is sure why. Was it disease? Was it an injury from one of his chariot rides? It's still a mystery today. Many scholars believe that Tut was assassinated by someone close to him who wanted his power. Maybe Tut was becoming too independent and would no longer listen to his advisors.

Whatever the cause of his death, it was a shock to the Egyptian people. The Egyptians believed that in order to preserve a person's *Ka*, or soul, the dead body had to be mummified and placed in a tomb. Since Tut's death was unexpected, the Egyptians had to work frantically to put together a tomb for their king. Inside the tomb, they placed items that would keep their king entertained and comfortable in the afterlife. Then they created false chambers and hidden passageways to lead robbers away from its many treasures. Three thousand years passed and shifting sands, grain by grain, covered the burial area—Tut's tomb vanished from sight.

Much of what we know today about King Tut's life comes from his tomb. In 1922, archeologist Howard Carter uncovered a buried chamber in an area of Egypt called the Valley of the Kings, where most of the pharaohs were buried. Behind a secret door Carter found the tomb of King Tut, almost perfectly preserved. It contained amazing artifacts—a golden mask and coffin, food vessels, jewelry, chariots, bows and arrows, statues of servants, game boards, furniture, and a magnificent throne.

X-rays of the mummified Tut show that he might have died from a head injury—more proof for those who think he was murdered. ❖

Among the treasures, Carter discovered a clay tablet with hieroglyphs on it that warned: "Death shall slay with his wings, whoever disturbs the peace of the Pharaoh." He also found a statue that read: "It is I who drive back the robbers of the tomb with the flames of the desert. I am the protector of Tut's grave." With his eyes on the other treasures, Carter quickly forgot the warning words until Lord Carnarvon, the man who had paid for the expedition, got sick and died two weeks after visiting the tomb. Some thought it was from malaria, but others believed it was King Tut's curse. Next, a friend of Lord Carnarvon visited the tomb. The following day he got a high fever and suddenly died! Soon all sorts of deaths were linked to the discovery of Tut's tomb. Within ten years of opening the tomb, almost thirty people connected to the excavation had mysteriously died.

Finally, Dr. Ezzeddin Taha, who had examined several people involved in the excavation of Egyptian tombs, noticed that many of them suffered from a strange fungal infection. His research revealed that some fungi could survive for up 4,000 years in mummies and tombs! Symptoms of the infection were a high fever and an upper respiratory infection. Ironically, after making this important scientific breakthrough, Dr. Taha died in a car crash. People today still debate whether Taha died because of the curse or because he had the fungal infection, which caused him to pass out and crash the car.

King Tut's death and tomb may be shrouded in mystery, but it is no mystery that, as one of the youngest pharaohs of Egypt, his memory lives on. His leadership and diplomacy skills helped strengthen Egypt's economy and return people's confidence in the pharaohs. His short life, his amazing tomb, and its curse have made him the most famous and well-known of all Egyptian kings. Like the ancient scribes of Egypt wrote, "Let your name go forth, while your mouth is silent." For no other pharaoh has this been more true than for King Tut.

Now, when I die,
don't think I'm a nut.
Don't want no fancy funeral,
just one like ole King Tut. (King Tut)

—FROM COMEDIAN STEVE MARTIN'S HIT SONG "KING TUT"

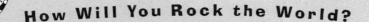

How Will You Rock the World?

I want to rock the world by being the world's greatest globe-trotting photojournalist AND athlete of all time! I was born in Barcelona, Spain (I am a citizen of the U.S. and a citizen of Spain). I have traveled to many places and taken many pictures with my dad's professional 35mm camera during my journeys. Although I enjoy photography and would like a career in this area, sports, namely basketball, is my first true love. I am already 6'1" tall, and I play ball EVERY DAY. One day I hope to play basketball professionally like my father AND take plenty of pictures while I am doing so!

Reginald Johnson, Jr., age 12

Galileo Galilei

1564–1642 ✤ *Inventor/First Physicist* ✤ *Italy*

Galileo, perhaps more than any other single person, was responsible for the birth of modern science…Galileo was one of the first to argue that man could hope to understand how the world works, and moreover, that we could do this by observing the real world.

—*NOBEL PRIZE-WINNER STEPHEN HAWKING*

Galileo was bored. After a week of studying math at the university, he had been looking forward to a good Sunday church service to fill his brain with more spiritual thoughts. Unfortunately, the visiting priest was so dull that Galileo couldn't keep his head from dropping onto his chest. Snapping it to attention, he overcompensated and threw his head back too far. Something on the ceiling caught his eye. A lamp, hanging from a chain high overhead, was swaying in the air currents. Its rhythmic arcs almost put him back to sleep, but then Galileo noticed something that surprised him: there seemed to be a pattern to the swings.

Wide awake now, he used his own pulse to time how long it took the lantern to swing from one end of its arc to the other. He realized something: each swing took the same amount of time, whether the lantern had swung wide in a new breeze, or had settled into a barely noticed sway when the air currents quieted.

Duh, you might say; that seems obvious. But it wasn't a *duh* then. People four hundred years ago had hardly a clue about what made the physical world work. With this observation, eighteen-year-old Galileo discovered the way to invent the first accurate mechanical clock, and began a lifetime of experiments to figure out how the world works. He was the world's first physicist (a scientist who studies matter and energy and how they interact).

Galileo's curiosity would nearly get him killed later in life, but it also started humans down the road of knowledge to mechanics, electricity, radiation and nuclear reactions. From a boring church service in Pisa in 1583 to a walk on the moon in 1969, and finally to nanotechnology today, there have been curious men and women, pulling more and more from the spool of scientific knowledge that Galileo started to unravel.

Galileo's greatness came from his skepticism: he refused to believe something just because everyone else did. He came by this naturally; as a boy, Galileo had been taught by his father, who hated close-minded people, especially if they were in a position of authority.

By the time he was eleven, his father could not keep up with Galileo's thirst for knowledge, so he sent his son to a monastery school. The peaceful life inside the monastery walls totally appealed to Galileo, so much so that, at thirteen, he volunteered to begin training to be a monk. His dad was horrified and instantly nixed the idea: Galileo needed to pick a career that would generate enough money to help support the family. And four hundred years ago, just like today, doctors got paid big bucks. So, at his father's insistence, when Galileo was seventeen he entered the University of Pisa to study medicine. But he was not interested in medicine, and argued with his father to be allowed to study math—a profession that would help him figure out how the world worked. He must have been a good arguer because his father gave in. As Galileo later said of his passion for math:

...the universe cannot be understood unless one first learns to comprehend the language and interpret the characters in which it is written. It is written in the language of mathematics, and its characters are triangles, circles and other geometrical figures, without which it is humanly impossible to understand a single word of it....

At Pisa, Galileo kept on arguing with people who supposedly knew more. He argued so much that his teachers nicknamed him *Il Attaccabrighe*, the Wrangler. What was he arguing about? Galileo felt that the facts they were teaching should not be accepted until someone had tested them.

Galileo said that a lock of wool and a piece of lead, if in a vacuum (with no air resistance), would fall at the same rate. In 1971, astronaut David Scott stood on the moon and dropped a feather and a hammer at the same time. They both fell side by side to the moon's surface. He remarked: "This proves Mr. Galileo was correct." ❖

When he was twenty-one, Galileo left school without earning a degree. Four years later, he was back, this time as an instructor. He began teaching math, and went back to his old argumentative ways. At that time, universities were still following the teachings of Aristotle, who had lived 1,800 years earlier. One thing Aristotle had said was that the heavier an object was, the faster it would fall. Aristotle had never actually tried it; it just seemed to logically flow from other things he had observed.

Galileo easily proved this idea wrong: he climbed the Leaning Tower of Pisa and dropped two lead balls, one weighing much more than the other. As his critics watched, an 1,800-year-old "truth" was overturned: both objects fell to the earth at exactly the same speed. By using public stages like this, Galileo became popular and changed many people's minds. But his popularity and ideas also created enemies, and he got fired from his job. Fortunately, friends got him a job at the University of Padua, near Venice. It had a reputation as being more open to new ideas, and Galileo was happy there. His fame grew as he invented and designed machines and instruments for various rulers and kings.

In 1609 the telescope was invented in Holland. It could magnify objects only up to three times, and was merely used as a toy at parties. But Galileo saw other uses for the telescope and set about to improve it. By 1610 he had made a telescope so strong it could be used in war to spy on approaching enemies. When he presented his telescope to the ruler of Venice, he was given a huge pay raise and a job for life. Orders poured in for his telescopes and he became even more famous. He used his most powerful scopes—ones that could magnify an object thirty times—to look at the sky and discovered that the moon is full of mountains and craters. He also discovered another thing Aristotle was wrong about.

Aristotle had claimed that the earth was the center of the universe—that the sun and all the other stars and planets revolve around the earth. And the powerful Catholic Church agreed with him. If the earth was the center of the universe, then that proved that the smartest creature on earth, *man,* must be the center of the universe as well. Anyone who disagreed with this idea was considered an enemy of the church. And, at that time, the church was the same as the government. The punishment for disagreeing with it was torture or death.

> The Catholic Church was very powerful in Italy in Galileo's day. In Rome, everyone was Catholic, and one out of every twelve people was a priest or a nun. ❖

Even though the Polish astronomer Nicolaus Copernicus had already said that the sun was the center of the universe, very few people believed him. Galileo did. His improved telescope allowed Galileo to prove that many of Copernicus's ideas were right. Galileo wrote a book, *The Starry Messenger*, arguing that the earth was *not* the center of the universe. Instead, he said the earth revolved around the sun. This book got him in big trouble. At age fifty-one, Galileo was forced to withdraw his ideas or risk death. To save his life, Galileo said that he had been wrong.

For the rest of his life, Galileo battled the church over his beliefs. They often threatened him with prison, torture, and death to force him to lie about his discoveries, but he never totally gave in. He always continued writing and teaching the truth, even when the pope and the Inquisition (the Catholic Church's secret police) came after him. For the last eight years of his life, Galileo had to live under house arrest inside his home in Florence—but he never stopped conducting his experiments.

Some heroes die rather than admit something that they don't believe in. Why didn't Galileo defend what he believed to the death? Maybe he wanted to live to make more discoveries. Or perhaps he knew that, whether he lived or died, the truth would eventually be known. And of course it was. Today everyone, even the Catholic Church, believes that Galileo was right.

In the end, Galileo's greatest legacy is not any one of his inventions or discoveries, but more his search for truth, even in the face of ignorant laws and rulers. In Galileo's day, the enemy of truth was people clinging to unproven beliefs. What is the enemy of truth today?

How Will You Rock the World?

My dream is to become an aerospace engineer and create exploratory vehicles that go to Pluto and Proxima Centauri. I might design public shuttles to the moon and Mars with fuel tanks that could be fastened on in case of fire, sleeping cabins close to the galley, oxygen, and food supplies, and nuclear-powered engines. The ejectable sleeping cabins would have ram motors—motors that magnetically attract the hydrogen thinly spread through space, and then burn it with an oxidizer. I could see it all now, me a famous aerospace engineer changing the way people travel.

Neil Forrester, age 10

Wolfgang Amadeus Mozart

1756 – 1791 ✤ *Composer* ✤ *Austria*

*I declare to you on my honour that he is
the greatest composer who ever lived.*

—JOSEF HAYDN, SPEAKING OF MOZART

Five-year-old Wolfgang could not hold it in anymore. All morning
the music had run through his head, and he just had to write it
down. He waited impatiently until his father Leopold went out for a coffee with a friend. Grabbing a quill and his father's inkwell and forgetting
that he had not yet learned to write, he filled a page with smudgy notes.

"What are you *doing*?!" Leopold burst in on the boy.

"I am writing a concerto. It will be done soon," replied Wolfgang
calmly, already sure of himself. Both men laughed and winked at each
other. How cute, they thought…the boy imitating his father, the court
composer for the Archbishop of Salzburg, Austria. But when Leopold

read the notes, he began to cry for joy. His tiny son had indeed written a complicated and well-organized concerto.

This ink-stained beginning was the first of over 600 pieces of music Mozart wrote, many of them complex symphonies he created in one sitting. He said that, before he wrote a single note, he heard the entire piece in his head, sometimes with as many as twelve different instruments. He wrote feverishly, perfectly, with no revising. Many people then and now consider Mozart to be the greatest composer the world has ever known.

Unlike today, when geniuses like Tiger Woods earn big money from competitions and endorsements, in Mozart's day talented people could only find success if they won the favor of royalty. Instead of being seen as artists, they were seen merely as craftsman, like a good carpenter or tailor. If you had talent then, your only hope was to be noticed and rewarded by your king or queen.

> Young Mozart charmed the Empress of Austria when he asked her little daughter, Marie, to marry him. Marie grew up to be the famous Marie Antoinette, Queen of France. Perhaps she should've married Mozart—she died at the guillotine when rebels overthrew the French monarchy. ❖

Mozart's dad, knowing that he had a child prodigy on his hands, saw young Wolfgang as the family's ticket to fame and fortune. So when Wolfgang was six, his father took him and his sister Nannerl, who was also talented, on a three-year tour of Europe. Dressed up as a miniature adult, complete with a powdered white wig, Wolfgang performed musical tricks like instantly playing any new piece given to him, or playing the harpsichord with the keys hidden under a cloth.

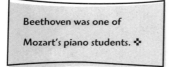

> Beethoven was one of Mozart's piano students. ❖

Wolfgang and Nannerl played for the kings and queens of Austria, France, and England, and everyone loved the talented children. Love, however, did not pay the bills, and Wolfgang's father was constantly frustrated by the stinginess of the royal families. They often would reward his children with nothing more than a golden snuffbox or some other small trinket.

When the family returned to Salzburg, the archbishop there accused

Mozart's father of writing all the music his young son had supposedly composed. The archbishop locked Wolfgang in a palace room for seven days and ordered him to write some music for the church. It took Wolfgang less

If you want to learn more about Mozart's life, check out the movie *Amadeus*. ❖

than seven days to produce a musical score of 208 sheets of paper. The archbishop was convinced. When he was just fourteen, Mozart wrote and directed his first opera.

Wolfgang spent his entire childhood touring, except for brief visits back to Salzburg, and time recovering from smallpox, typhoid and other illnesses. These illnesses probably contributed to his early death. By age twenty-one, Wolfgang had traveled all over Europe, composing and performing sonatas, concertos, symphonies, church music, music for string quartets, and opera for kings and queens.

It is easy to think that geniuses have it easy. But with music flowing out of his fingertips as fast as most people form a sentence, Mozart had to answer to people who saw him as a freak of nature, a person who didn't have to work hard:

> *It is a mistake to think that the practice of my art has become easy to me. I assure you, dear friend, no one has given so much care to the study of composition as I. There is scarcely a famous master in music whose works I have not frequently and diligently studied.*

Despite his genius and amazing devotion to his craft, as an adult, Mozart usually could not scrape together enough coins to pay for food, fuel or rent. He was often at the mercy of stingy noblemen who took advantage of his skills while paying him little, and ordering him to write what he considered to be boring, uninspired pieces for their parties. When he did finally find a patron, he couldn't even ask for a decent salary, but instead had to humbly

Once a friend stopped by Mozart's apartment and found him and his wife waltzing wildly. "What are you doing dancing with no music?" he asked. "Keeping warm," answered Mozart. The couple had no money for firewood. ❖

take whatever was offered. He also had to suffer the embarrassment, even though he was praised as the most divinely inspired composer ever, of being seated at the servants' table.

Even though the times he lived in made it hard to earn money, Mozart compounded his own problems: when he did have money, he blew it. Have you ever noticed that the smartest kid in class can never find his calculator or your brilliant mother is always losing her purse? Sometimes the smartest people seem to have gaping brain-holes for the more practical matters of life. That was Mozart. Because he was so bad at making and keeping money, Mozart never earned enough to relax. Instead of being able to compose music, which was all he wanted to do, Mozart had to teach piano most of the day, perform at small parties in the evenings, and then squeeze in his composing in during the very latest hours.

> Mozart's whole name was Johann Chrysostomus Wolfgang Gottlieb Mozart. Gottlieb means, in German, "God-loved." After dropping the first two names, and changing Gottlieb to its Latin synonym (*ama*=love; *deus*=God), he was known as Wolfgang Amadeus Mozart.
> ❖

Mozart worked nonstop and grew weaker and more exhausted as he got older. At thirty-five he received a fearful omen: a mysterious stranger appeared at his door and asked him to write a requiem mass (a funeral song). The stranger would not reveal his identity, and as Mozart worked on the requiem, his health got worse and worse. He became convinced the stranger was a messenger from God and that he was writing his own funeral music. He was. Mozart died before the piece was finished.

Mozart was famous in his lifetime and even more famous today. There has never been another genius like him. The music that poured out of Mozart over 200 years ago is still played, in television commercials, in movie soundtracks, and of course in concert halls. You may not know you know Mozart, but you do; his music is all around us.

Louis Braille

1809 – 1852 ✤ Teacher/Inventor ✤ France

The blind can now work, they can study, they can sign, they can add their share to the good and happiness in the world. It was Louis Braille who found the golden key to unlock their prison door.

–HELEN KELLER

The instructor tapped on his desk, calling the reading class to order. But this was no ordinary reading class. The embossed books used by the French Royal Institute for Blind Youth in 1819 were so special that the school owned just fourteen of them. This was ten-year-old Louis' first day in class and he was thrilled: he would finally be able to read on his own!

Embossed books for the blind had been invented 30 years earlier. To make them, large letters were pressed into thick sheets of waxed paper, leaving impressions. Then, when the page was turned over, the letters could be read by tracing their outlines with a finger. The only problem was, each page could hold just a few sentences, so the books were big and fat. You couldn't even hold one, but had to prop it up on an easel.

Still…it was reading, and after the seven years of darkness since he'd lost his sight, Louis was excited. But his excitement soon turned to disappointment. Louis found that tracing each letter with his finger took so long that by the time he got to the end of a sentence, he couldn't remember what it said at the beginning. Even if he could remember what he was reading, what good did it do? In all of France, there were just a handful of embossed books. They were too expensive to print and too big to store.

There must be a better way, Louis thought. For years the problem occupied his mind, and ultimately evolved into the greatest gift to blind people that has ever been invented: a reading system known simply as braille, for the boy who invented it. Without braille, the blind would never know the joys of losing themselves in a good novel or even reading sports scores—the daily tasks that sighted people take for granted.

> When Louis first experimented with sonography, he eagerly discussed his ideas with Captain Barbier. Barbier was not pleased to have his design questioned—especially by a kid! He insisted that it could not be changed. Good thing Louis didn't listen to him! ❖

Louis Braille lost his sight at age three, when he accidentally poked his eye with a tool in his father's harness-making shop in Coupvray, a small village 25 miles from Paris. The eye became infected, and when little Louis rubbed it, he accidentally spread the infection to the other eye as well. Within weeks of the accident, he was totally blind in both eyes.

His father made him a cane that allowed him to explore his physical surroundings, but the cane could only take him so far into the world. His blindness left him isolated: he couldn't play games, run through the woods or climb trees with the other children. And two hundred years ago, the blind were thought to be mentally handicapped. People figured that if a person couldn't see, he or she couldn't think either. Blind people weren't welcome in schools or taught any trade or skill. If you were blind in Europe back then, you'd probably end up a beggar on the streets.

Luckily, the village priest in Coupvray saw Louis for what he was: a normal boy who happened to be blind. Fr. Jacques Palluy taught him and convinced the schoolmaster to accept Louis as a pupil. As if to make up for his lack of vision, Louis's memory was phenomenal, and he learned rapidly. So rapidly that Fr. Jacques was able to get him into the Royal Institute for Blind Youth in Paris.

Today Louis Braille rests in the Pantheon in Paris, the burial place of France's greatest heroes. ❖

At the school Louis read his first books and acquired skills that would allow him to support himself. When he was thirteen, the institute had an important visitor, a man who would change Louis's life. Charles Barbier was a retired captain in the French army who had invented a military code based on dots and dashes punched with a *stylus* (a sharply pointed, pen-like tool) into strips of cardboard. The code allowed field commanders to silently give orders like "Advance" or "Withdraw" at night. When it occurred to Barbier that blind people might find it useful, he expanded his code so each word was broken into sounds and each sound was a different combination of dots and dashes. He called it "sonography" or "sound-writing."

Sonography looked complicated, but the school's director agreed to try it. Louis became a sonography expert, but the more he learned about it, the more problems he found: since the symbols represented sounds, there was no way to show spelling, punctuation, or numbers. And many of the symbols were too big to read with the single touch of a finger. Sonography was so hard to use, many blind students gave up.

eBraille is now being developed. It's a web-based system to transcribe and deliver any web page or computer file into braille to users anywhere. ❖

Louis didn't give up, but began experimenting with sonography. From age thirteen to fifteen, his days were filled with classes and friends, but at night and on weekends he created patterns of dots, trying to find an easier system. Some nights, Louis lost track of time; as he sat on his bed punching dots, the rumbling of wagons outside told him that morning had come. His passion took a toll on his health, and he developed tuberculosis.

Then one night, as his classmates snored away, a brainwave hit Louis: the *sounds* were the problem. He had been stuck trying to work within

Barbier's system when it was the system itself that was wrong. Instead of representing sounds, Louis created symbols that stood for the *letters* of the alphabet. Just like the alphabet sighted people use. His code was made up of six dots, like this:

This code unit, called the "braille cell," has space for six dots: two across and three down. For each letter of the alphabet, mark of punctuation, symbol, and number, Louis worked out a different arrangement of dots. Here's how his first name looks in braille:

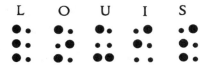

Every letter and symbol could fit within the space of a fingertip. When he demonstrated his invention for the school's director, Dr. Pignier, he asked him to read aloud a paragraph from any book: "Read slowly and distinctly, as if you were reading to a sighted friend who was writing down your words." As Pignier read, Louis punched holes with his stylus onto a sheet of paper. It was so easy to do that he told Dr. Pignier, "You can read faster." Pignier finished reading and Louis finished "writing" at almost the same time. Then, as the amazed director watched, Louis turned the paper over and read, with his fingertips, the raised bumps his stylus had left—every word Dr. Pignier had dictated. The man was overwhelmed with emotion. He knew what this meant: a fifteen-year-old boy had just switched on the light of learning for blind people forevermore.

During the next few years, Louis improved and added to his system. At twenty, his system perfected, he wrote a book explaining it, called *Methods of Writing Words, Music, and Plain Song by Means of Dots, for Use by the Blind and Arranged by Them.* The braille system solved the main problems of the earlier embossed books. Since braille letters could fit under a person's fingertip, it was possible to read much faster. Braille letters took up about the same space as printed letters, so the books weren't so huge and expensive to produce. And best of all, because braille was like the regular alphabet that sighted people used, it was easy to learn.

Despite Dr. Pignier's enthusiasm, government officials were slow to change. They didn't want to give up their old embossed letter system, and asked, "Why should blind people learn a different alphabet than the rest of us?" Obviously, they never had to read their embossed books! When Louis's school got a new director, even he refused to use braille. But so many students were smuggling styluses into the school and teaching each other braille, the new director had to give in.

> At the school for the blind, Louis also learned to play musical instruments. He was so good that for the rest of his life he earned a living playing music in Paris churches. ❖

Louis stayed at the institute his entire life, teaching and playing music. When tuberculosis overtook him, at forty-three, his last words were, "I am convinced that my mission on earth is finished."

Imagine a life without reading: no Internet, no computer games, no Harry Potter. Thanks to the invention of a teenage boy, millions of blind people only have to *imagine* that kind of a life...they don't have to *live* it. Thanks to Louis, they can open a book, anytime, and read whatever they want. The horrible accident that blinded Louis Braille also gave him the will to create one of mankind's most humanitarian inventions.

Crazy Horse

1841–1877 ✤ *Sioux Warrior/Leader* ✤ *North America*

One does not sell the earth upon which the people walk.

—CRAZY HORSE

Thirteen-year-old Curly was shocked. He had just seen U.S. troops shoot Chief Conquering Bear in the back while he was negotiating with them for peace. These white men cared little for the Sioux or their way of life. They slaughtered buffalo for sport, introduced new diseases that the Sioux had no protection against, and sold them whiskey, which made them sick. Curly hoped that a vision from the Great Spirit, *Wakan Tanka,* would show him how to help and protect his people.

For three days, Curly laid down in an isolated spot on the prairie—no food, no shelter—praying for a vision. To keep awake, he lay on sharp stones. By the third day without sleep, Curly was exhausted. He was weak from hunger and his body was sore from the rocks. And still, *Wakan Tanka* had not given him a vision.

Pulling his aching body up off the ground, Curly searched for his pony. Suddenly, the air grew hazy. A great warrior appeared, riding a pinto similar to Curly's own horse. Most Sioux warriors carried scalps as war trophies, but this warrior had none and wore only a single feather in his hair. Behind the mysterious rider, storm clouds gathered. Gunfire and arrows rained from the sky and a lightening bolt shot down, grazing the warrior's face. Then, as quickly as he appeared, the strange warrior melted away. Though Curly didn't realize it then, this vision would change his life forever. Curly would one day become the rider in his dream—a fearless warrior and champion for the Sioux. People far and wide would know him as Crazy Horse.

The Sioux believed buffalo were sacred animals and when they killed one, they used every part of it—the bladders became water bags, bones became tools and knives, and hides became blankets, clothing, drums, and tipis. White settlers, on the other hand, paid $10 to ride a buffalo-hunting train. In one day on the train, a single person could shoot over 100 buffalo—which they just left to rot! In 20 years, more than 30 million buffalo were massacred. By the 1900s, the great buffalo herds were gone. ❖

Born in 1841 in South Dakota's Black Hills, Crazy Horse was first named Curly because of his wavy, light-brown hair. Curly's mother died when he was a baby, and his father was a holy man. As a young child, his Sioux tribe rarely stayed in one place for more than a few days because they followed the buffalo herds. Sioux riders were outstanding horsemen. They were so skilled on their pintos that they could fight, hunt, and *even sleep* on horseback!

By the time he was fifteen, Curly was a great horseman and hunter, but his true destiny was still unclear. To gain insight into Curly's future, Curly and his father built a sweat lodge. Sioux sweat lodges were usually small tents built around a pit containing hot rocks, and were used to gain self-awareness, purification, and higher knowledge. Curly, who had never told anyone about his vision, finally revealed to his father what he had

Curly was a great buffalo hunter. He crafted a bow for himself with arrows made of porcupine quills. He located herds by placing his ear to the ground and listening to the thunder of their hooves in the distance. While an experienced hunter was lucky to shoot just one buffalo during a hunt, Curly killed two on his very first trip! ❖

seen two years earlier. His father told him that one day he would be a great warrior—the dream rider in his vision. After several years of training, seventeen-year-old Curly was ready to go to battle. To protect him, Curly's father made a special medicine powder of dried aster flowers and eagle's brain, which Curly was to put in his mouth and rub on his skin. Curly also wore a red-backed-hawk feather and painted a lightening bolt down his nose to represent the warrior in his vision.

Curly's first battle was between the Sioux and the Arapaho over land rights. After several hours of fighting, the Sioux were losing ground. Suddenly, Curly and his horse raced through enemy gunfire and arrows, and shot two Arapaho warriors. As soon as Curly saw the second warrior fall, he reached down to scalp the man for his war trophy, a symbol of his skills as a warrior. At that moment Curly was shot in the leg! Though he wasn't severely injured, he had learned his lesson: to become the dream rider of his vision, he should not take the scalps of his enemies.

When Curly returned to the Sioux camp, stories were circulating about how he had almost single-handedly won the battle. The whole tribe held a victory dance in his honor. Curly, a quiet boy, downplayed his tremendous role in the battle. To honor his son for his bravery, Curly's father announced to the tribe: "My son. . .has done a brave thing; for this I give him a new name. . .Crazy Horse." For the next seventeen years, Crazy Horse fought in many battles. His reputation as a warrior grew, and he became famous far and wide as a great Sioux leader and war strategist.

In 1875, a U.S. government commission was sent to meet with the chiefs from several tribes. The commission demanded that the chiefs sign a new treaty that would give almost all of the Sioux, Cheyenne, and Arapaho land to the U.S. government. For three days the chiefs discussed what they should do. When the commission returned, accompanied by

120 U.S. soldiers, they were shocked to discover themselves surrounded by 7,000 warriors. The land negotiations failed and the result was all-out war.

Though not all the Sioux wanted to fight, Crazy Horse saw no other option. He remembered the death of Conquering Bear, who had been so unfairly shot, and declared, "For me, there is no country that can hold the tracks of the moccasin and the boots of the white man side by side." It was time for war. In 1876, Cheyenne forces joined the Sioux to form an army and fight U.S. forces. In one of their first major battles, later called "Custer's Last Stand," just forty Indians were killed, compared to the deaths of General Custer and 220 U.S. soldiers. The Sioux strategy was brilliant, combining surprise attacks with detailed knowledge of their land.

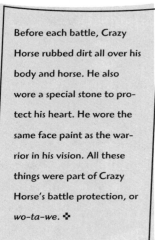

Before each battle, Crazy Horse rubbed dirt all over his body and horse. He also wore a special stone to protect his heart. He wore the same face paint as the warrior in his vision. All these things were part of Crazy Horse's battle protection, or wo-ta-we. ❖

This taste of victory didn't last long, however. Outnumbered by the U.S. troops and low on supplies and weapons, the Sioux were in serious trouble. Some warriors fled with their families, but many stayed with Crazy Horse to continue fighting. Unable to get more food or supplies because of the war, many in the tribe grew sick. Crazy Horse, worried for the welfare of his people, made a difficult choice: he decided to surrender.

In 1877, Crazy Horse marched into Fort Robinson with 800 followers to give himself up. A group of Sioux, who had surrendered earlier, were waiting for them and sang out in strong voices welcoming their leader. One soldier commented, "By God, this is a triumphal march, not a surrender." Even though they'd lost the battle, the Sioux were proud they'd stood up and defended their land and their way of life. General Clark, head officer of the fort, shook the hand of the great warrior, and Crazy Horse said, "I have been a man of war and have always protected my country against invaders. Now I am for peace. I will… fight no more."

Though most Sioux greatly admired the courageous warrior, a few were jealous and did not like Crazy Horse. They spread rumors that he was planning to murder General Clark. When soldiers arrested him, Crazy Horse tried to escape and was stabbed with a bayonet. That night, at age thirty-six, Crazy Horse died. The next day, soldiers went to bury the body but Crazy Horse's friend, Touch of Clouds, pulled a gun on them. Touch of Clouds brought Crazy Horse's body to his father for a traditional Sioux burial. Legend says that every night, until Crazy Horse was buried, an eagle paced across his coffin. Crazy Horse's father buried the body, not telling a soul of the grave's location.

Up to the very moment of death, Crazy Horse fought bravely, staying true to his vision and becoming the great Sioux warrior and protector of his people he had always dreamed of. Today, a memorial to Crazy Horse is being carved out of a mountainside in the Black Hills, a permanent reminder of Crazy Horse's heroic life.

How Will You Rock the World?

I want to be a photographer for a nature magazine. I would like to take really interesting pictures of misunderstood or feared species and write articles about why we should respect them like any other animal. My role in this would be to provide the knowledge it takes to convince people to stop fearing strange animals and to start to know just how beautiful they truly are. Whether they're winged or clawed, scaled or finned, they are all wonderful, fascinating forms of life and need to be recognized as their true selves, not as monsters or nightmares, but as fellow creatures that can amaze us if we just take the time to discover them.

Cameron Livermore, age 12

Thomas Alva Edison

1847-1931 ✢ *Inventor* ✢ *United States*

Genius is one percent inspiration and ninety-nine percent perspiration.

—THOMAS EDISON

When fifteen-year-old Tom walked into the offices of *The Detroit Free Press* to buy the newspapers he would sell later that day, he was met by a worried crowd. It was 1862, and the Civil War battle of Shiloh was underway. There were vague reports that hundreds of men had been killed. Tom sold papers and snacks on the train between Detroit and Port Huron, Michigan, but the mood in the office gave him a new business idea: people wanted information about the war and he would *sell* it to them.

At the train station he asked the telegraph operator to wire a bulletin about the Battle of Shiloh to the stationmaster in each town the train

Tom created the world's first "invention factory" in Menlo Park, New Jersey. The men who worked there were as thrilled to be on the cutting edge of technology as Bill Gates must have been when he invented his first computer operating system! ❖

would stop at on its way back to Port Huron. Tom asked the stationmasters write down the battle report on the station blackboard. Then he went back to the newspaper office and convinced them to give him 1,000 papers, instead of his usual 100, promising to pay them the next day. On the train that day, just as Tom had thought, people read the blackboard bulletins and wanted more information. At first he sold papers to them for five cents, but by the last stop people were so eager for news that he sold the papers for a quarter each! He sold every paper that day, and learned a valuable lesson: an idea that is useful to a large number of people can make you money!

Thomas Alva Edison was born in 1847; at birth, his head was so alarmingly big that the doctor said he had a "brain fever." Must have been all those brains, because by the time he died, in 1931, Thomas Edison held 1,093 patents for inventions, the most of any American inventor. (A patent is a certificate that gives an inventor exclusive rights to use or sell his or her invention, and keeps other people from stealing the idea and making money from it.) Two of his most famous inventions were the phonograph (the ancestor of today's CD and tape players), and the electric light bulb.

After that day on the train, when the telegraph helped Tom make money selling newspapers, he was hooked on it. He began working as a telegraph operator in his teens. The telegraph, ancestor of the telephone, was operated by turning an electric switch off and on at different rates to create a clicking sound that was transmitted over a wire. Each letter had its own click sound and telegraph operators had to translate the clicks into English for the person receiving the message. It was the first electric form of long distance communication.

The telegraph did have one big failing, however. It couldn't send a message more than 200 miles. If a message had to travel more than that, it had to pass through many

Tom nicknamed his first two children Dot and Dash after the telegraph signals. ❖

stations, where each operator listened to the message and then sent it to the next station. With all those people interpreting the clicks, the final message often sounded nothing like the original. (If you've ever played the game "telephone," you understand the problem.) While working as a telegraph operator, Tom solved the problem. He fixed a machine so that it could receive a message and send it on automatically. Instead of a reward for this bit of genius, he was fired. His supervisor had been working on the very same problem and wasn't too happy being upstaged by a nineteen-year-old.

But getting fired was no big deal to Tom. He really wanted to spend his time inventing anyway. He began writing down all of his ideas, his experiments, and their results. (When he died, he had filled over 3,400 notebooks!) Tom was so excited about his many ideas, he wrote, "I am twenty-one. I may live to be fifty. I have got so much to do, and life is so short. I am going to hustle." His first invention was an automatic vote counter. It worked perfectly. Only problem was, no one wanted it. It was the first and last time Tom would work on an invention that people didn't need. Like today's entrepreneurs, he only wanted to invent things that were needed.

> Tom even invented a primitive "photocopier." You wrote with an electric pen on a special sheet of waxed paper. Instead of ink coming out, the pen made tiny holes, turning the paper into a stencil. Then ink was pressed through the stencil to make more copies. ❖

Penniless at twenty-one, he moved to New York City where his friend, Franklin Pope, let him sleep in the back room of a Wall Street business. After the workers went home, Tom spent his evenings snooping around until he had figured out how all the equipment worked. One day the office exploded in chaos: the "ticker" machine that sent minute-by-minute gold prices to clients had broken. As angry clients crowded into the office, Tom told the frantic boss he could fix the machine. "Fix it! Fix it!" the boss screamed back. Within hours, Tom fixed it so that the problem would never happen again. That success encouraged him to open a business with his friend. Pope Edison & Company's motto was to "devise electrical instruments and solve problems to order."

By twenty-three, Tom had already earned tons of money on his improved ticker machine and was on his way to a lifetime of inventions. It wasn't all easy: often in the early years he went broke when an invention didn't work, and he spent over $2 million defending his patents against people who tried to steal them. But by the time he was thirty-nine, he was a millionaire, ready for the most important—and the favorite—invention of his life.

When Tom worked the midnight shift as a telegraph operator, his boss made him prove he was awake by sending a telegraph every hour. Tom promptly rigged up the machine to automatically signal his boss every 60 minutes, while he snoozed away! ❖

In 1876, Alexander Graham Bell invented the telephone. It converted the human voice into electric signals. Then, at the receiving end, the electric signals were converted back into a voice. It was scratchy and was hard to hear, but it worked. Tom, of course, wanted to make it better.

While trying to improve the sound quality of the telephone, Tom stumbled upon something else altogether. He used the telephone's diaphragm (a flexible disk that vibrates with the sound of a voice) and a pin to put the sound waves of human speech on paper: "I rigged up an instrument and pulled a strip of the paper through it at the same time shouting, 'Halloo!'" The sound vibrated the diaphragm, causing the pin to mark the paper. Then, when he pulled the paper through the instrument again, the pin's marks activated another diaphragm. A ghostly "Halloo!" was heard. "I was never so taken aback in all my life," recalled Tom. He had just invented the phonograph—the ancestor of today's CD players. You can thank Thomas Edison next time you pop in your favorite CD.

Yeah, CDs are important, but Tom's next big thing *really* changed the world. Like many other inventors at the time, Tom was obsessed with creating an electric light. He bragged that he would soon be able to light up lower Manhattan, but it wasn't as easy as he expected. For over a year he searched for the right material for the filament (the threadlike part of the light bulb that glows), trying different metals and even bamboo fibers. Lucky for Tom, his labs were filled with odd pieces of minerals, plant parts, tools, rocks—just about anything he thought might be useful. Tom believed "the most important part of an experimental laboratory is a big scrap heap." In that "scrap heap" the perfect filament was finally found.

Back then, oil lamps were used for light; when the lamps burned, they left a black residue, *carbon*, on their glass globes. Tom was absent-mindedly rolling a bit of this carbon, called "lampblack," between his fingers when he suddenly realized it might make good material for the filament. He was right. And the first light bulb was born.

It took three more years for crews to tear up streets and walls in a ten-square-block area of New York City to put in electrical wiring. Although it wasn't quite "lighting up all of lower Manhattan," when Tom threw the switch to turn on 800 lights in twenty-five buildings, no one complained! Tom's thoughts on that day: "I have accomplished all I promised." The electric age had begun!

Over the rest of his long life (he lived to be eighty-four years old), Tom continued to work on inventions. Unlike some inventors, whose ideas are known only to experts, Thomas Edison always wanted to make things that were "useful" to everyone. He was never content to accept things as they appeared—his genius was to find a better use for a machine, or a way for it to work better. His ideas paved the way for the thousands of electronic tools, games and entertainment we have today. Seventy years after his death, his influence is still felt as we live an electrified life, one full of useful inventions that sprang from the brain of Thomas Edison.

How Will You Rock the World?

I will rock the world by revolutionizing air transportation. I will design an aircraft that can cross any ocean in record-breaking time. I will also design a spacecraft that is cheap and efficient and can fly people into outerspace on a regular basis. I have already designed a ship that will travel to Mars!

Kwame Anyika, age 12

George Washington Carver

1865 – 1943 ✤ Botanist ✤ United States

*It has always been the one
great ideal of my life
to be of the greatest good to the
greatest number of my people possible.*

—GEORGE WASHINGTON CARVER

The farmer tried everything to get his corn to grow better—more water, different fertilizers—but nothing worked. He was at the end of his rope.

"Take this to the Carver place," he said, handing a small, sickly-looking corn stalk to his son, "Give it to the Plant Doctor."

The farmer's son had to walk miles to get there and when he finally found the Plant Doctor, his jaw dropped open in shock. George Washington Carver, dubbed the "Plant Doctor" by his neighbors, was just eight years old! Yet, when young George took the unhealthy plant, he spoke with great confidence: "Don't worry. I'll put this in my garden and try some things out on it. I'll figure out what's wrong."

When the farmer himself returned to the Carver place a few weeks later, he couldn't believe his eyes. Like magic, his small, wilted corn plant was now tall, green and healthy. "Here's what you do…" and the young scientist described a new kind of fertilizer he'd created that would make the farmer's sick corn grow like crazy. The man shook his head in wonder: *How could a boy know so much about plants?*

Eventually, this eight-year-old "Plant Doctor" of Missouri would grow up to become the "Plant Doctor" to the entire United States. His inventions would change the very food we eat and his ideas would help poor farmers grow successful crops and rise from poverty. He would become one of the most famous and respected scientists in the world!

It might be hard for you to believe, but this scientific genius was actually born into slavery! George Washington Carver and his mother were owned by Moses and Susan Carver. When George was still a baby, he and his mother were kidnapped by greedy Confederate raiders who planned to sell them out of state to the highest bidder. The Carvers offered a reward to get them back, but only George was found. The thieves had left the baby behind when they realized he was sickly. George's mother was never seen again.

The neighbor who found and returned baby George to the Carvers was given a horse as a reward. ❖

From that day on, the Carvers raised George and his brother, not as slaves, but as their own children. George was small and frail, but he knew that while his body might be scrawny, his brain was brawny. He was fascinated by nature and spent all his free time collecting things to study: plants, rocks, dirt. . .even bugs and frogs. He collected so much that the family built him an outdoor shed to keep it all in. By the time he was eight, George knew so much about nature that his neighbors went to him for advice. He experimented on sick plants in his secret garden in the woods until he made them healthy again.

More than anything, though, George wanted to go to school.

When just a mere tot. . .my very soul thirsted for an education. I literally lived in the woods. I wanted to know every strange stone, flower, insect, bird, or beast.

Although everyone in town knew how smart George was, the school for white children wouldn't let him in. Unlike today, when all kids in America, black and white, can go to public schools for free, George had no way to learn. Can you imagine wanting to learn so badly that you would walk hundreds of miles, sleep in barns and work for your food, just to go to *school*? Well, that's exactly what George did when he was only twelve years old! He set out on his own to get an education. He would find a school that would take him, work to pay his way and learn all the teachers knew, then take off again to find smarter teachers!

> While George was traveling around getting an education, he lived for a time in a house he built himself. . .out of dirt! His sod house was so well-built, all the neighbors asked for George's help building theirs. ❖

Going to college was George's big dream. It took him years of hard work and travel, but at age thirty he finally finished enough classes and was the first African-American accepted to Iowa State College of Agricultural and Mechanic Arts. Even though he was officially accepted into the college, George still battled fear and prejudice on campus. He was forced to eat meals in the basement instead of in the dining hall with the other students. With quiet dignity, George held his head high, worked hard, and forced the students and faculty to face their racist attitudes. Before long he was truly accepted everywhere white students went and made many friends.

> Inventor Thomas Edison asked George to be his research partner and offered him a very high salary, but George turned him down because he felt the students at Tuskegee and the farmers in the South needed him more. ❖

At long last the Plant Doctor's dreams came true when he earned his master's degree in Agriculture. Though he was offered many teaching jobs at white colleges, George chose to teach at the Tuskegee Normal and Industrial Institute in Alabama, a college for African-Americans. Their Agriculture Department didn't even exist before George arrived, so he and his students had to build everything from scratch, including their classroom! George taught his students to reuse everything they found— discarded bottles became beakers and jar lids were melted down for chemicals to experiment with. Their department supplied all the food for the entire school, so they quickly learned the most efficient, cheapest ways to grow and manage their plants and animals.

George teaches farmers to recycle! At Tuskegee, George was thrilled to continue some of the research he started as a boy. All around him he saw problems facing poor farmers, so he put his brain to work fixing them. Many farmers couldn't afford fertilizer, so George taught them to put their dead plants into a big pile, which eventually rotted down into free fertilizer! Nowadays we call this *compost.* You may even have a compost pile at *your* house. Feeding farm animals was also expensive, so George invented animal food made from acorns, which grow plentiful in the South and can be collected for free.

George saves the soil! The Plant Doctor helped out farmers even more with his discoveries about cotton. This was the main crop grown in the South back then, but it quickly sucked up all nutrients in the soil. After a few years of growing cotton, farmers couldn't grow anything else in their exhausted fields. George discovered that certain plants actually put nutrients *back into* the soil. He taught farmers to use "crop rotation," planting cotton one year, then a crop like peanuts, soybeans or sweet potatoes the next, to put nutrients back into the soil and make their fields healthy again.

George goes crazy with peanuts! The farmers didn't know what to do with these strange new crops, so George did some more experiments and invented over 300 uses for the peanut! He made peanut milk, butter, coffee, shampoo, dye, paint, paper, plastic, and even chop suey sauce! Then he invented 100 ways to use the sweet potato—everything from chocolate to paste to ink. Thanks to George, everyone uses crop rotation now, and peanuts, sweet potatoes and soybeans are three of the most popular and profitable crops in the South!

> Peanuts were brought to America from Africa with the slaves, who called them goobers. Peanuts were used mostly to feed animals; humans didn't think much of eating them until George came along. ❖

> The U.S. government was so impressed with George's achievements, they named a submarine after him and put his face on a stamp and the half-dollar. ❖

George had many passions. He loved art so much that he almost gave up science to become a painter. He painted on everything—cans, scraps of paper, the walls, the floor. One of his paintings, *Yucca and Cactus*, was even displayed at the 1893 World's Fair in Chicago. ❖

George's ideas became so popular that soon farmers, black and white, from all over the South, were asking his advice. His reputation spread quickly, and in 1918, the U.S. government invited him to the capital to tell them about his ideas. His brilliant work was starting to make him famous and he won tons of awards…even from beyond the grave! In 1990, almost fifty years after he died, George became the first African-American to be inducted into the National Inventors Hall of Fame.

Even with all the fame, George preferred the simple life. Unlike many scientists today who make millions when they patent their inventions, George never asked for or earned *any* money from his many discoveries. He believed his ideas were given to him by God and should be shared with others for free. If people sent him checks for his help, he returned them. George worried that if he earned lots of money he would get so busy taking care of the money that he wouldn't have time for research. He

Henry Ford, inventor of the assembly line, was such an admirer of George that he built a school and a museum named after him. ❖

was so devoted to science that he never married either. When asked why, George answered, "How could I explain to a wife that I have to go outdoors at four o'clock every morning to talk to the flowers?" He was quite happy with his research, knowing he was helping the world.

George continued his teaching and research at Tuskegee up until the very day he died in 1943. At his funeral, President Franklin Roosevelt sadly remarked, "The world of science has lost one of its most eminent figures. . .his genius and achievement [were] truly amazing." So, next time you eat a peanut butter and jelly sandwich or spread fertilizer over your garden, maybe you'll think of the young Plant Doctor and his unstoppable dreams.

Pablo Picasso

1 8 8 1 - 1 9 7 3 ✤ *Artist* ✤ *Spain*

Every child is an artist.
The problem is how to
remain an artist once he grows up.

—PABLO PICASSO

Fifteen-year-old Pablo looked up from his easel. The bowl of grapes he was painting seemed to stare back at him. Rubbing his eyes, Pablo examined his "still life": each grape was supposed to look perfectly realistic, but instead they just looked flat and lifeless on his canvas. He wanted to capture how the fruit *really* looked. . .but how? The rest of the day, Pablo experimented with various brush strokes until he finally came up with a new technique he was happy with.

That evening, Pablo's father, José Ruiz, a well-known painter and art teacher, returned home from his classes. José was most famous for his paintings of pigeons—in fact, most people thought he was the best pigeon painter in all of Spain! "Did you complete your painting, Pablito?" José asked. Pablo nodded, nervously pointing to the still life drying in the studio. What would his father think of his new technique? José only stared in amazement at Pablo's work. *What's wrong?*, Pablo wondered. Finally José said, "My son, you have surpassed my talents—I can no longer paint in the shadow of such work."

From that day on, Pablo's father stopped painting completely—even pigeons! His son Pablo, however, would go on to paint many more masterpieces. . .most of them not in the realistic style José so greatly admired. Unlike most artists, who become famous only after they die, Pablo Picasso would enjoy great fame while he was still alive. His paintings would revolutionize the art world and be celebrated worldwide!

Painting may have come easily for Pablo Picasso, but he faced many struggles in his early years. Born on October 25, 1881 in Malaga, Spain, Picasso was horribly shy as a child and a real "underachiever." Even though he didn't excel socially or academically, his mother Maria told him, "If you become a soldier, you'll be a general; if you become a monk, you'll end up as the pope." Whatever Picasso's career in life, she was sure he would achieve greatness.

Because his father was an art teacher, Picasso was introduced to painting at an early age. When he was only ten, he completed his first major painting, revealing a talent well beyond his years. By the time Picasso was fourteen, he took the entrance exam for the Academy of Fine Arts in Barcelona. For older students, the grueling exam took at least a month, but Picasso, a child prodigy, finished it in just one day.

While at the academy, Picasso excelled in his work and refined his painting technique, but was unhappy with his teachers' narrow-mindedness when it came to art. At fourteen, Picasso painted *The Old Fisherman.* Because the painting was not *exactly* realistic, Picasso's instructors disapproved. Picasso changed art schools and by age sixteen was winning praise and honors, but his style was still criticized as being too different. Picasso was not happy. He wanted to express himself freely!

Frustrated with his painting career in Spain, nineteen-year-old Picasso moved to Paris. Paris was then the center of the art world, a place where artists could break away from traditional styles. Picasso blossomed, exploring "abstract" styles of painting. If he saw a painting he liked, he would try to copy the artist's style and learn from it. Soon he was able to reproduce the techniques and styles of famous painters like Degas and Monet, but he still hadn't found his *own* artistic style.

> During his Rose Period, Picasso so loved the circus that he went three or four times a week! ❖

Picasso's artistic breakthrough finally came to him by way of a tragedy: his best friend committed suicide. Picasso went into a deep depression and his art reflected his mood. He began painting people on the edge of society—beggars, prostitutes, the physically disabled—using mostly blue and gray colors. The paintings were unique and totally different from anything Picasso had done before. This time period, from 1901-1903, is now called Picasso's "Blue Period."

Picasso's paintings changed again in 1904, this time thanks to love. He met Fernande, a beautiful, red-haired artist's model. As his grief lifted with his new relationship, Picasso started painting in pink, rose, and earth tones instead of dark, depressing colors. He also focused on a new subject matter: colorful circus performers and other artists like himself. This period was later called Picasso's "Rose Period."

> One of Picasso's most famous cubist sculptures is in downtown Chicago. Built in 1967, the gigantic steel sculpture is 50 feet tall, and some art critics believe that Picasso used his dog as the model for it! ❖

As his work was gaining fans in Paris, Picasso started exploring other creative techniques. Instead of using color to make his paintings different, he studied African art and experimented with geometric shapes. From these forms emerged the style that Picasso is now famous for: *Cubism*. People were shocked by Picasso's wild new paintings, which were so abstract it was hard to tell what was going on. They looked as if they had been shattered, like glass, and then put back together the wrong way. Though many people criticized the strange new paintings, others marveled at Picasso's creativity. Cubism was soon the talk of the town. Demand for Picasso's work grew quickly and it wasn't long before his paintings were worth thousands, then millions, of dollars!

Even though Picasso is most famous for cubism, he continued to experiment with his style throughout his life. A prolific painter, Picasso would sometimes paint three or four masterpieces in a single day. He created thousands of works of art, including paintings, stage set designs, book illustrations, sculptures, ceramics, prints, and collage. One of his most famous paintings was *Guernica* (1937), which Picasso painted to protest the cruelty of the Spanish Civil War. To Picasso, art was his way of fighting society's injustices.

Picasso painted until the end of his life, finishing one final self-portrait just before he died at the age of ninety-one. The son of a painter of pigeons, Picasso grew up to be one of the wealthiest and most praised artists in the world. From the highly realistic work of his youth to his more famous cubist paintings, Picasso has inspired art lovers like no one else.

How Will You Rock the World?

My dream is to become an illustrator of books. I love to draw and create images that come alive on paper. This will rock the world because I will turn words into pictures and become a

famous illustrator. I want to create a whole new technique for illustrating that explains things as well as words can. This will help people visualize their world in a whole new way.

Daniel Solow, age 11

Albert Einstein

1879 - 1955 ✤ *Physicist* ✤
Switzerland/United States

*Imagination is
more important than knowledge.
Knowledge is limited.
Imagination encircles the world.*

—ALBERT EINSTEIN

Albert took a breath of fresh mountain air as he walked up the steep slope. Ahead of him was Professor Winteler, one of the few teachers Albert liked, and several classmates. Professor Winteler often took his students on hikes in the Swiss Alps. Staring at the sunlight reflecting off the snowy hills, Albert's mind drifted. *What would it be like if people could travel at the speed of light?* he wondered. Lost in thought and not paying attention to the path, Albert suddenly tripped and slid toward the edge of a cliff! Just before tumbling down the mountain, Albert grabbed onto some icy rocks and a friend reached out to him with his walking stick.

"Thanks!" Albert said, grabbing the stick, "You saved my life!"

It wasn't the first time scientific questions distracted Albert Einstein, and it wouldn't be the last. Later that same year, sixteen-year-old Albert wrote his first scientific paper titled, *On the Investigation of the State of Ether in the Magnetic Field.* The paper brought up questions that were burning in Albert's mind and that many scientists had never considered before. It paved the way for his future as one of the most remarkable scientists in human history, a man whose theories would transform the way we perceive the universe.

> Einstein's Theory of Relativity came to the shocking conclusion that time, weight and mass are not constant. When moving at high speeds, all of these things get compressed; only the speed of light remains the same. That happens because energy is equal to mass times the speed of light squared, or $E=mc^2$. ❖

When Albert Einstein was born in Ulm, Germany in 1879, the first thing his grandmother said was that he was "much too fat! Much too fat!" Albert's head seemed abnormally large and his family was worried there might be something seriously wrong with him. But Albert grew up to be a healthy and fairly normal young boy. His father, Hermann Einstein, sold feather beds for a living and his mother, Pauline, cared for Albert and his little sister Maja. Albert's mother encouraged him to explore and question the world as much as possible. At five, Albert was given a compass to play with while recovering from an illness. Fascinated by the needle's movements, Albert realized that there was some force making the needle point always in the same direction. Suddenly he realized there was "something deeply hidden . . . behind things."

Albert's curiosity ruled him, but it also made it difficult for him to concentrate in school. He would constantly daydream about nature's "hidden" forces. When he spoke in class, his teachers thought he talked too slowly. Soon they began calling him *Herr Langweil*, which translated means "Mister Stupid." Even the principal said that Albert wouldn't amount to anything. But for Albert, it was nearly impossible to pay attention in class, which consisted mainly of memorizing facts—kids weren't even allowed to ask questions!

> In his free time, Einstein loved to play the violin and sail. ❖

Then, one day, Albert's life changed forever when a family friend gave him a geometry book to read. In a short time, twelve-year-old Albert had read the entire book and finished all of its equations. Soon Albert was reading as many science books as he could get his hands on, books like *Force and Matter* and *Kosmos*. By the time Albert was thirteen he had finished *A Critique on Pure Reason* by Immanuel Kant, a complicated theoretical book that even some professors had a hard time understanding. According to one family friend, "Kant's works, incomprehensible to ordinary mortals, were clear to [Albert]." Although Albert's teachers still considered him an idiot, it was becoming apparent to the Einsteins that their son had a unique perspective on the world.

Albert struggled through high school, but finally graduated and entered a technical school in Switzerland. At twenty-one, he finished his degree but couldn't get a teaching position, so he eventually settled for a job at the Swiss Patent Office. Albert liked the work because he could learn about new inventions and spend his free time thinking about physics. He did a lot of thinking during his first three years at the patent office and came up with his now-famous "Theory of Relativity" (otherwise known as $E=mc^2$). The theory had to do with such enormous concepts as how humans understand time, space and reality. Einstein's idea was radical and completely tossed out other established theories.

> Though Einstein was admired for his intelligence, he was also extremely absent-minded: he constantly lost his keys, his clothes never matched or fit right, he would even forget to eat! ❖

The scientific community was astounded. How could a lowly patent clerk come up with such a revolutionary theory in physics? Even though Einstein's theory was controversial, his brilliance was finally recognized. He was offered and accepted a professorship first in Prague, Czechoslovkia and then in Berlin, Germany, and was the youngest person ever invited to the world physics conference in Belgium. Einstein enjoyed teaching, and both professors and students traveled from across Europe to hear him lecture. By 1919, Einstein's career was skyrocketing. That year, scientists in England proved Einstein's theory correct! News of the discovery circled the globe and Einstein became world-famous. In 1922 he was awarded the Nobel Prize for physics. What his elementary school teachers must have thought!

But physics wasn't Einstein's only passion. He was also a pacifist—a person who believes fighting wars is wrong. Living in Europe, he had witnessed the devastation of World War I and could sense that a second World War was brewing in Germany. He protested against the German government, but to no avail. Hitler and the Nazi party, racist and political extremists, were gaining more control over the country and limiting the rights of Jewish citizens. Einstein, who was Jewish, feared for his life (indeed, by the end of the war, the Nazis had killed millions of Jews). He fled to the United States in 1933, where he became a professor at Princeton University.

By 1939, Hitler had invaded neighboring Poland, and World War II was under way. Einstein was worried that the Nazis would use his theory, $E=mc^2$, to create an atomic weapon that would help them win the war. He wrote to President Franklin Roosevelt recommending that the U.S. fund research on atomic weapons. As a pacifist, this must have been a difficult decision for Einstein to make. But the threat of a world ruled by the Nazis terrified him even more. President Roosevelt agreed and a group of physicists began working on the "Manhattan Project," a top-secret mission to create an atomic bomb.

Though Einstein's formula $E=mc^2$ was key to the project, he was not directly involved. On August 1945, America dropped atomic bombs on Hiroshima and Nagasaki, Japan (Germany's ally). The bombings certainly ended the war, but they also killed over a hundred thousand innocent Japanese civilians. Einstein never got over the use of the bombs, and for the rest of his life he advocated for peace. He declared: "Peace cannot be achieved through violence, it can only be attained through understanding."

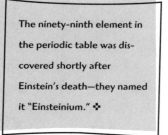

Television and fluorescent lights came from Einstein's discovery of the Photoelectric Effect, a theory that proved that light could act like waves and like particles. ❖

The ninety-ninth element in the periodic table was discovered shortly after Einstein's death—they named it "Einsteinium." ❖

During his life, Einstein was also part of the Zionist political movement, which wanted to form a new nation for people of Jewish descent. The group's efforts resulted in the creation of the country Israel in 1948. In 1952, Israel's president Chiam Weizmann died, and Israel offered the presidency to Einstein! Though Einstein was honored, he declined, explaining that he was too old and inexperienced for the job.

Three years later, Einstein died from heart failure. Near his bed were several unfinished equations. What was Einstein trying to figure out in those last equations? We may never know. What we do know is that Einstein was one of the world's most remarkable men—a physics genius, an advocate for peace, and a Jewish role model and leader. But to all this, Einstein would probably say, as he said before, "I have no special gift. . .I am only passionately curious."

How Will You Rock the World?

My dream is to be a magnificent biologist who would study the dynamics of life. I will research how living cells work, live, and reproduce and their environment. My inspirations are Bill Nye and Albert Einstein and I wish I could be like either of these marvelous scientists. Two of the things I want to accomplish as a biologist are to stop animal AIDS and find a new, unknown organism.

Lucas Sprague, age 12

Jesse Owens

1913–1980 ✤ *Olympic Athlete* ✤ *United States*

The minute you think you've got it beaten, you're beaten. No matter what you did yesterday, each sunrise wipes the slate clean.

– JESSE OWENS

Twelve-year-old Jesse Owens ran every race full out, as if he were running the 100-yard dash. That day in 1926, he was running the 220-yard dash against some of the best junior high runners in Cleveland. As usual, Jess had pulled ahead of his competition at the start of the race. But, as was happening more and more often, runners inched by him on the track. When he finally reached the finish line, the tape was already fluttering in the breeze, broken by someone else. Today he came in third place. What was he doing wrong?

Jesse was so mad, he continued running at full speed until he plowed into the brick wall surrounding the track. Bouncing off, dazed and hurt, he looked up from the grass and saw Coach Riley looking down at him.

"Congratulations, Jesse! You won today. Even when the race was over, you didn't stop." Jesse thought his coach was making fun of him for running into the wall, but he was serious. Even though Jesse was still making the same mistakes he made the last year, his coach knew Jesse could be a champion. In that single display of fierceness, Coach Riley saw in Jesse the character and determination of an Olympian.

Back in 1926, this was a radical idea. Jesse was black and poor, and the Olympics were not exactly friendly to black athletes. Jesse's own dad, beaten down after a life of hard labor and discrimination, didn't want his son to get his hopes up for the Olympics. He told Jesse, "It don't do a colored man no good to get himself too high, 'cause it's a [long] drop back to the bottom." But Coach Riley was right to dream big for Jesse, because ten years later, Jesse Owens stood in front of the world and accepted *four* Olympic gold medals in track.

Jesse Owens was born James Cleveland Owens in 1913 in Alabama to sharecropping parents. The life of a sharecropper was miserable—not much better than a slave's life. So, when the big cities of the North, like Detroit, Chicago and Cleveland, began making cars and machines, and hiring tons of workers, millions of blacks left the farms of the South, hoping to find a better life. Jesse's parents moved to Cleveland, Ohio when Jesse (or J.C., as he was known then) was eight.

When he got to Cleveland, right from the start Jesse was at a disadvantage. Schools for blacks in the South were so bad that, by age nine, Jesse could barely read or write. He was put in the first grade, where he couldn't fit into the tiny school desk. On his first day of school when the teacher asked his name, he replied, "J.C., ma'am." Misunderstanding his Southern drawl, the teacher wrote down "Jesse," and he was too intimidated to correct her.

His poor beginnings in school meant that he would struggle with his

> Jesse's honesty and fairness were legendary. In one meet, his archrival stumbled off a rickety starting block. Jesse easily won the race, but insisted it be re-run so his opponent had a fair chance. Jesse lost the second race, but showed everyone the real meaning of being a good sport. ❖

studies all the way through college. But there was one place where he excelled: on the track. "I always loved running," Jesse said. "It was something you could do under your own power. You could go in any direction, fast or slow…fighting the wind…seeking out new sights just on the strength of your feet and the courage of your lungs."

In middle school, Jesse met the man who would change his life—Coach Riley. Because Jesse had to work after school to help support his family, he couldn't make it to regular track practices. So, Coach Riley worked with Jesse early in the mornings before school started. He became Jesse's mentor, on and off the track.

> Today's tracks, with their bouncy surface, give runners a lift, and are made to drain water away so it doesn't form puddles. But in 1936 tracks were made from crushed cinders (pieces of partly burned coal). When it rained, the runners' heavy leather shoes soaked up the muck from the soggy track, slowing them down. ❖

For a while, Jesse lost most races, even though he was faster than anyone else. Before each race, he was doing the 1920s equivalent of trash-talking: staring his opponents down, trying to intimidate them before the race. Coach Riley watched in silence. It was only when Jesse asked, "Why can't I win?" that day he crashed into the wall, that his coach did a peculiar thing. Instead of answering, he drove Jesse to a racetrack to watch horses run. "What do you see on their faces?" Coach asked. "Nothing," Jesse answered. "That's right," Coach Riley noted, "Horses are honest. No animal has ever tried to stare another down…horses make it look easy because the determination is all on the inside where no one can see it."

From that day on Jesse put his emotions aside when he ran, concentrated on his body—not his opponents—and tried to run like a horse, with an easy, fluid and graceful power. He started winning!

At fifteen, he began setting world records for his age. He ran the 100-yard dash in eleven seconds. At eighteen, he became the high school world champion in the long jump; and at nineteen, he broke the world record for the 220-yard dash, at 20.7 seconds. Jesse, along with his teammate, David Albritton, another future Olympian, helped their school earn first place in the most prestigious high school track meet in the Midwest. They came back to Cleveland as heroes. They were even welcomed by a parade.

Jesse, now a nationally ranked athlete, was recruited by Ohio State to run on its track team. Unlike today, when some college athletes are treated like campus royalty, attending school for free and living in luxury, in the 1930s, poor athletes had to work full time to pay for their education. Jesse worked three jobs while going to class and competing.

Despite being one of Ohio State's biggest stars, Jesse was still discriminated against. Because he was black, he couldn't live on campus, or eat in the restaurants close to school. When he and his teammates traveled to competitions, the whites rode in separate cars from the black athletes. In many gyms, the blacks weren't even allowed to take a shower. Jesse was frustrated that even though his white teammates were friendly, they did nothing to protest this racist treatment. As Jesse said, "Their niceness didn't include making sure you got to take your shower too." But those hard times helped strengthen Jesse's character and prepared him for the difficult challenges to come.

After an incredible season in 1935 where, in one day, Jesse smashed three world records and tied a fourth, he began thinking he might actually make it to the 1936 Olympics. Sure enough, a few months later he was chosen for the U.S. Olympic track team and hopped a ship to Europe for the Olympics. That year, they were being held in Nazi-controlled Berlin. The Nazis hated Jews and blacks and other groups that they called "non-humans." The pressure was on the German athletes to show that Hitler was right when he claimed that the Aryans (white, blue-eyed, blond-haired people) were the "master race." And just as much pressure was on the United States, with its ten black athletes, to show how wrong Hitler was.

Jesse felt the pressures of competition, race, and his incredible fame at the Olympics (where he awoke one morning to a hoard of autograph seekers thrusting their arms through his open bedroom window). But he

Jesse was finally honored by the president for his accomplishments at the 1936 Olympics—forty years later! President Gerald Ford awarded him the Medal of Freedom, the highest honor our country can pay to a civilian in peacetime. ❖

In Berlin, the street outside the Olympic Stadium has been renamed Jesse Owens Strasse (street). ❖

remembered Coach Riley's lesson. He kept his emotions in control, and won four gold medals for the U.S. in the 100-meter dash, long jump, 200-meter run, and 400-meter relay. He also won the hearts of the German fans with his grace, sportsmanship and awesome speed. And, just like he'd learned to do at home, he ignored Hitler's racism. He even became friends, much to Hitler's anger, with Germany's top track star, Luz Long. The world loved Jesse, not just for his running, but for keeping his cool under tough circumstances.

Despite his star status, life wasn't easy when Jesse got home. As a black man in America, most doors were closed to him. When he couldn't find a job to support his wife and family, he was forced to humiliate himself by racing against horses for pay. His first real job was as a playground instructor earning $30 a week—not a lot of money even then. But over the years, as America's racism eased and Jesse's achievements were recognized, life got better. He counseled young people, taught sports clinics for the government during World War II, and started his own public relations agency. In the 1970s he became an activist for racial equality, fighting for equal housing laws for blacks, and, as an advisor to baseball's American League, pushing team owners to hire black managers.

Despite Jesse's struggles against racism, he lived his life with dignity, never returning hatred with hatred, and always trying to change people's minds by his own fairness and honesty. He said:

> No matter how much bad there is, the best way to get rid of it is to expose the good. Don't just hack away at the roots of evil. They go all the way to China. Plant next to prejudice another tree that grows so big and high that discrimination has to wither and die.

Nelson Mandela

1918– ✤ Activist/Nobel Peace Prize Winner ✤
South Africa

The struggle is my life.
I will continue fighting for freedom
until the end of my days.

—NELSON MANDELA

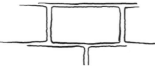

The crowd hushed as the chief began speaking: "We are here today to celebrate our sons becoming men." Rolihlahla glanced at the other teenage boys. Like him, they were painted from head to toe in white earth to symbolize their purity for this coming-of-age ceremony. For weeks they'd been living in grass huts apart from their families. Now their whole village was here to celebrate their return as men. He couldn't wait to see what gifts he would get. Some sheep? Maybe even a cow or two of his own?

He snapped back to attention as the chief's voice turned angry, "We promise them manhood, but it's a promise we can't fulfill. For we Xhosas, and all black South Africans, are a conquered people." He pointed at the boys: "Here are chiefs who will never rule because we have no power to govern ourselves; scholars who will never teach because we have no place for them to study." He looked at the proud families and finished sadly, "These gifts we bring them today are nothing, for we cannot give them the greatest gift of all: freedom and independence."

Rolihlahla thought about the chief's words as he ceremonially burned the grass hut filled with his boyhood belongings. His uncle, his mother, his whole village expected him to become a chief. But he was beginning to see there were some things more important than becoming a chief. He wanted to help his people fight for equality with the white man. That day he realized he would have to leave his village and his father's wishes behind. In fact, he would have to leave his entire childhood behind. Rolihlahla shivered as he watched the flames devour the hut; not from the cold, but from his own fear of the future.

Rolihlahla had good reason to be afraid. Ever since whites had landed in South Africa hundreds of years before, they had stolen land from black Africans and prevented them from having any power in the government.

As a child, Nelson loved to herd cattle and hunt birds with a slingshot. He was also excellent at stick-fighting, a traditional African sport. ❖

There were five times as many black people as whites, yet blacks were allowed to keep only 13% of the land in the country—and only the very worst land. Rolihlahla would grow up and risk his life fighting these injustices. He would become known as Nelson Mandela, the most famous prisoner in the world, and would sacrifice his own freedom to lead his people and his country into a new future.

Nelson was born in 1918 in a small village and his father was a chief of the Thembu people, who are part of the larger Xhosa tribe. At birth he was named Rolihlahla, which means "troublemaker." Little did his parents know how much trouble their son would make one day! When Rolihlahla started school, a white teacher couldn't pronounce his name. "From now on, your name is Nelson," she told him. The name stuck.

His father had hoped Nelson would become a chief, but he died when his son was just nine. Nelson's mother knew it would be difficult getting an education for her son without her husband's help, so she sent Nelson away to be raised by a family friend, Jongintaba, the head chief of all the Thembu people. Nelson was sad to leave, but he was quickly accepted as a part of Jongintaba's family and was treated just like a son in the royal household.

Nelson's passion for justice was born as he watched the chief settle tribal disputes. While the white government made laws without giving black people any say, Thembu chiefs listened to all members of the tribe and a decision was made only if everyone could

> Nelson was so poor when he arrived in Johannesburg that he often walked the twelve miles round-trip to work just to save on bus fare. ❖

agree. Nelson wanted to bring that kind of justice to all South African blacks, not just his own tribe, so he decided to become a lawyer instead of a chief.

After his coming-of-age ceremony, Nelson left his village to attend an all-black university. When he and other students protested the school's white rule, the principal asked them to stop and most students gave in. Nelson wouldn't back down, however, and got kicked out. He knew Jongintaba would be furious, so he ran away to the big city: Johannesburg.

Johannesburg, which was built around diamond mines, attracted thousands of black people from the countryside who were looking for work. Blacks weren't allowed to live near whites, so they had to live in areas outside the city called townships, crowded together in tiny, tin-roofed shacks with dirt floors, no running water, no heat, and no electricity. Nelson was shocked by the poverty and the racism that caused it, but he was also excited about the political activity going on around him. Other black Africans were fighting back. They had created the African National Congress (ANC) to demand their human rights and equality.

Nelson signed up and soon became one of the ANC's leaders.

And just in time. In 1948, the white government turned the unofficial rules separating blacks and whites into formal law, called apartheid. Apartheid means "apartness" and the new laws kept the races separated. Whites had total control. "Whites Only" signs went up everywhere, forbidding blacks to use buses, restaurants, beaches, etc. Blacks had to carry identification with them at all times. They were told where to live, work, and go to school. They were forbidden to marry anyone outside their race. If they broke an apartheid law, they went to jail.

Nelson planned protests, boycotts of white-owned businesses, and mass strikes, which thousands of blacks took part in. By refusing to work, shop, ride buses or go to school, black Africans peacefully shut the city down. While he was protesting, Nelson was also busy getting his law degree. In 1952, he and a friend, Oliver Tambo, opened Johannesburg's first black law firm: Mandela & Tambo. They were immediately swamped with clients. Nelson describes a typical morning:

> *We had to move through a crowd of people in the corridors, on the stairs and in our small waiting room. Africans were desperate for legal help: it was a crime to walk through a Whites Only door, a crime to ride a Whites Only bus, a crime to be unemployed and a crime to be employed in the wrong place, a crime to live in certain places and a crime to have no place to live.*

During the 1950s, black Africans lost more and more rights every day. In 1960, the fight against apartheid turned violent when 5,000 blacks gathered to protest in a township called Sharpeville. Even though the protesters were peaceful, white police opened fire on them and mowed down 69 innocent people—most of them shot in the back as they tried to run away. The rest of the world was horrified by the violence. But instead of loosening the apartheid rules, the government cracked down harder. Now blacks couldn't be on the streets after sundown and couldn't gather in public at all. The ANC was outlawed.

In prison, communication between the political prisoners was often forbidden. They got around this rule by writing and passing secret notes on toilet paper. ❖

After the Sharpeville Massacre, Nelson felt that it was time to try other methods. Many blacks were getting killed during "peaceful" protests. He decided it was time to fight back. As an ANC leader, he urged the use of force against *symbols* of apartheid—government buildings, railroads, factories—but not against *people*. When bombs started going off, it didn't take long for the police to figure out who was behind them. In 1963, Nelson and other ANC leaders were arrested and put to trial.

People around the world awaited the verdict. Nearly everyone was sure the ANC leaders would get the death penalty. Nelson wasn't afraid, however, and said to the court:

> *During my lifetime I have dedicated myself to the struggle of the African people. I have cherished the ideal of a democratic and free society…It is an ideal which I hope to live for and achieve. But, if needs be, it is an ideal for which I am prepared to die.*

To everyone's surprise Nelson and the others were not sentenced to death, but instead, to spend the rest of their lives in prison on Robben Island.

Robben Island Prison was a lot like the prison at Alcatraz Island in California—prisoners could see the mainland, but escape was impossible: the freezing water surrounding the island was filled with sharks! Nelson refused to lose his fighting spirit. His first day in prison a guard ordered him to jog. He refused. When the guard threatened Nelson, he growled back, "If you so much as lay a hand on me, I will take you to the highest court in the land, and when I finish with you, you will be as poor as a churchmouse." The guard never bothered him again.

Although the prisoners spent their days crushing stones into gravel or digging pits, Nelson kept their minds sharp. He successfully demanded that the prison create a library. Each day, while they worked, the prisoners taught each other all they'd learned about history, politics, philosophy, economics, etc. Many of them finished high school and college while in jail. Soon the prison was nicknamed "Mandela University."

As life in South Africa continued to get worse for black Africans in the 1970s and 80s, and as their clashes with whites grew increasingly violent, the name Nelson Mandela spread around the world, drawing attention to the horrors of apartheid. A song by Bruce Springsteen and Miles Davis called "Free Nelson Mandela" was a huge hit. Daily protests in American and European cities pressured governments to boycott South Africa—people stopped buying their diamonds, companies pulled out of the country and foreign banks stopped loaning money to the government.

Isolated from the rest of the world, and its economy in shambles from boycotts, the South African government had no choice. It offered to free Nelson if he promised to stop the violence. But the government still wasn't promising to end apartheid, so Nelson rejected the offer. After more than twenty years in jail he refused to leave until apartheid was gone and *all* black Africans were free. In 1989, as the world grew more and more disgusted with South Africa, a new president, F.W. de Klerk, was elected—he immediately began secret negotiations with Nelson.

De Klerk surprised the world on February 11, 1990, when he suddenly announced the end of apartheid and set Nelson Mandela free after twenty-seven years in prison. Together they began the difficult process of creating a new, democratic South Africa for all people, regardless of their color. In 1993 they were jointly awarded the world's highest honor, the Nobel Peace Prize, for working to end apartheid. A year later, for the first time in South Africa's history, blacks and whites voted together in democratic elections. After a lifetime of fighting for freedom and equality, Nelson was elected president of South Africa.

It was no easy job. He somehow had to bring blacks and whites together. He refused to take revenge on whites, and instead focused on creating a new future together while improving housing, education and employment for black Africans. At the 1995 Rugby World Cup, tens of thousands of white fans cheered "Nelson, Nelson" as their President walked onto the field in a team jersey. A fellow political prisoner explains the importance of the appearance, "The liberation struggle…was about liberating white people from fear. And there it was, fear melting away." Nelson understood that it would take both blacks *and* whites to repair the broken country.

After centuries of inequality, life in South Africa is still not perfect. But the changes that have taken place since the end of apartheid are amazing. Blacks can live, work and study wherever they want. They are free to follow their dreams. The "Whites Only" signs are gone. And it was Nelson Mandela who sacrificed most of his life to see those changes happen. He is a symbol of the dreams and struggles of oppressed people everywhere. His is the boy who could have been chief of his village, but who instead became a hero for the world.

How Will You Rock the World?

I want to rock the world by using my writing and public speaking skills as a tool for becoming a peacemaker. Life is so fragile and so temporary that we shouldn't waste time fighting. It's easy to care about people we know personally. What's sometimes difficult is to care for people we don't know about. If we can learn to be respectful of the unique differences we find in other people, we can then learn that there are so many similarities among us.

Mattie J.T. Stepanek, age 11

The Dalai Lama

1935 – ✤ *Spiritual/Political Leader* ✤ *Tibet*

For as long as space endures,
and for as long as living beings remain,
until then may I, too. . .
dispel the misery of the world.

—THE DALAI LAMA

The mud hut was dark and cold, with only a yak-oil lamp lighting the room. The traveling merchants couldn't believe that this shabby house in such a remote village might be the right one, but they carefully laid out dozens of objects just in case.

"Show us the things that belong to you," whispered the oldest merchant to a small boy. The boy's parents were bewildered as their son picked up a drum and then some old prayer beads.

"It's mine. It's mine," he said confidently each time.

The merchants raised their eyebrows at each other—the items had belonged to their dead leader. The boy chose correctly. "Perhaps we have found him after all," they secretly hoped.

Their hearts sank, however, when the boy struggled over his final choice. He stared at two nearly identical walking sticks, but couldn't choose between them. Everyone in the room held their breath. Were the earlier choices just a coincidence? As they began to give up hope, the boy smiled and took hold of the correct cane. The adults let out sighs of relief.

"The prophecies were correct," the old merchant cried joyfully. "We have found our Dalai Lama!" The boy's parents gasped in surprise as the merchants removed their disguises. The "merchants" were really high officials from the holy city of Llasa, and after years of searching they had finally found the next god-king of Tibet.

The young Dalai Lama was very mechanical. He could fix clocks and watches like a pro. He rebuilt an old car and raced it around the palace courtyard (there were no roads in Tibet!), and even started his own movie theater with a broken-down projector and some old newsreels. ❖

Tibet, located high in the Himalayan mountains between China and India, is a Buddhist country. Followers of the Buddhist religion believe in *reincarnation*: when a person dies, their soul is reborn into another living form. You could come back as a person, an animal, or even a bug! They also believe that their leader, the Dalai Lama, is always the reincarnation of the original Dalai Lama, who ruled Tibet in the 1300s. When a Dalai Lama dies, they must find the new child his soul has been reborn into.

Just like Cinderella and the glass slipper, when the 13th Dalai Lama died, officials scoured the land looking for his reincarnation. Meanwhile, in a small village in northeast Tibet, the future Dalai Lama, Llamo Dhondrub, was born in 1935. Although he was raised as a normal boy, he was always different. As soon as he could talk, the unusual boy told everyone that his home was really in Llasa and demanded to sit at the head of the table, instead of his father!

Before being discovered as the Dalai Lama, one of Llamo's favorite pastimes was hanging out in the chicken coop, pretending to be a chicken. He even sat on the nests! ❖

Back in Llasa, the monks' search for their reincarnated leader was guided by a vision. Looking into the waters of a sacred pool, they saw a temple with a blue roof and a house with strange wooden rain gutters. After years of searching, they finally found the temple and the house—it was the home of two-year-old Llamo.

After testing the boy with the belongings of the previous Dalai Lama, the monks took their new leader and his family to the city of Llasa where he moved into the Potala Palace. While *you* might be psyched to move into a palace with a thousand rooms, the Dalai Lama was bummed out. The stone palace was dark and cold—like a dungeon—and his family didn't live there. Worst of all, there were no other kids. His playmates were old monks and he made pets out of the mice that lived in his room!

> As a boy, the Dalai Lama was a bit of a troublemaker, but the monks couldn't punish him. How could they spank their holy ruler? When he got into trouble, they spanked his brother instead, hoping this would make him feel guilty enough to stop! ❖

The Dalai Lama lived this lonely life until he was fifteen. That's when his country was invaded by China, and he had to grow up fast. For hundreds of years, Tibet and China had argued about whether Tibet was its own country or just part of China. In 1950, China settled the debate by invading Tibet. The teenage Dalai Lama, who was still training to lead the country, was put in charge two years early to deal with the crisis. He hoped other countries might help, but no one wanted to anger China, a superpower, just to help out tiny Tibet. The Dalai Lama was on his own.

He struggled to lead his country, but life in Chinese-occupied Tibet got worse and worse for its people. Buddhist temples were destroyed and hundreds of monks were sent to prison, where many were tortured, starved and killed. Farmers were sent to work camps and their lands were given to Chinese immigrants. Although Buddhism forbids violence

> Whenever the Dalai Lama left Potala Palace, he was carried in a small room on poles, called a palanquin, and was followed by a parade of over 100 people, the palace horses and even cages of birds! ❖

and Tibet had no army, the people tried to rebel in 1959. They were no match for the huge Chinese army, and their rebellion was crushed.

After the failed rebellion, Tibetans feared that the Chinese would kill their Dalai Lama next, so they surrounded his palace, creating a human shield. It was a weeklong standoff. Even after Chinese soldiers fired shots into the crowd, they still would not leave. The Dalai Lama realized his people would give their lives to protect him. He couldn't just sit by and watch his country fall apart and innocent people die.

He planned a James Bond-style escape. His only hope was to get help from the outside world. But how? The palace was surrounded, Chinese soldiers were everywhere, and he would have to travel for weeks through the frozen Himalayas to get to the nearest country. In the dark of night, disguised as palace guards, he and his advisors sneaked out of the palace and into the crowd. Miraculously, no one recognized their sacred leader without his glasses on!

> In the years after the Dalai Lama's escape, Buddhism and the Tibetan language were outlawed. Punishment for keeping a picture of the Dalai Lama was death! Over a million Tibetans have been killed. When the Dalai Lama left, there were almost 3,000 Buddhist temples in Tibet. Now there are just nine! ❖

This was just the beginning of a terrifying two-week horseback journey through enemy territory. The hard travel, lack of sleep and bad food soon took its toll: most of the party got very sick, including the Dalai Lama. He was so ill that he couldn't walk, and he had to be strapped onto the back of a yak to finish the trip.

When they finally crossed the border into India, the Dalai Lama knew his adventure was over and the real work was just beginning. He founded a Tibetan community in the town of Dharamsala, high in the Indian Himalayas, a place where he and his people could practice their religion freely for the first time in ten years. In 1963 he also created a new and improved Tibetan government and their first democratic constitution.

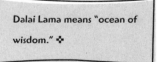

> Dalai Lama means "ocean of wisdom." ❖

Forty years have passed since the Dalai Lama's escape and Tibet is still not free. Chinese immigrants now outnumber Tibetans, and the country's ancient religion and traditions are practiced only by the escaped Tibetans now living in Dharamsala. The Dalai Lama has spent the past four decades traveling the world to protest this injustice. In 1989

In 1996, a Seattle, Washington, boy was discoverend to be the reincarnation of a Tibetan lama. At age two, the boy was taken to a Buddhist monastary in Nepal to begin his studies. ❖

the world heard his message: he was awarded the Nobel Peace Prize. World leaders, Hollywood celebrities, and the media have begun to speak out for Tibet and put pressure on China to change their policies.

While he has not achieved all of his goals, the Dalai Lama *has* saved the soul of his people. His Tibetan community in India is thriving, and in spite of China's power, the world knows about Tibet's struggle. In a world that often seems to be filled with war and hatred, the Dalai Lama reminds us that we *can* resolve our conflicts peacefully, if we choose to. The boy who grew up trapped inside a palace has spent the rest of his life traveling the world spreading his message of peace.

The problems we face today—violent conflicts, destruction of nature, poverty, hunger and so on—are mainly problems created by humans. They can be resolved—but only through human effort, understanding and the development of a sense of brotherhood and sisterhood. –THE DALAI LAMA

Elvis Presley

1935 – 1977 ✤ *The King of Rock 'n' Roll* ✤
United States

Before Elvis there was nothing.

–JOHN LENNON

The young singer gripped his guitar, but his hands still shook. Man, was he nervous! He looked around at the acoustic tiles on the ceiling, the tiles on the walls, the big microphone in front of him. He couldn't get over it. . .he was finally in the famous Sun Recording Studio. Sure, he had paid the studio $4 to make a record for his mom's birthday. Sure, they didn't know who he was. But this was *Sun Records*, where the most famous country and blues stars recorded. Anyone could be listening. Maybe this would be his big break.

"Who do you sound like?" asked the woman in the recording booth. "I don't sound like nobody," he answered with a grin. She chuckled at the sweaty teen with his weird long hair and sideburns, but as he belted out the songs, his gravelly voice grew on her. On a piece of scratch paper she scrawled: *Good ballad singer. Hold.* After he left, a woman in the waiting room asked her, "Who was that singing?" "I don't know," she answered, "Just some kid." "Well, whoever he is, he gives me goosebumps!"

She wouldn't be the last woman to get goosebumps from listening to Elvis Presley. Soon he would become the most famous singer the world had ever heard. Women would scream and tear their hair out whenever he opened his mouth. This nervous, greasy-haired kid would become the King of Rock 'n' Roll.

The King grew up dirt poor. The Presleys lived in a two-room "shot-gun shack" (named because you could open the front and back door and shoot straight through the house) in Tupelo, Mississippi. His mother Gladys worked picking cotton, and his father Vernon did odd jobs when-ever he could find the work. One January night in 1935, Gladys went into labor as sleet rained down. She was too poor to afford good medical care and her baby, Jesse Garon, died in the early morning hours. As the doctor was getting ready to leave, he was shocked to discover a second baby on the way. Just as Elvis was born, the black clouds over Tupelo parted and the morning sun shined through. The Presleys were sure it was a sign: God must have a plan for their son.

Even as a toddler, Elvis loved music. He lived in a mostly black com-munity and grew up listening to his neighbors' music. Gladys also took her son "church hopping" on Sundays to hear the beautiful gospel music of the South. "Some of those spirituals had big, heavy rhythm beats like a rock-and-roll song," Elvis said later, describing how church music influ-enced him.

Tragedy hit the Presleys when Elvis was still a young boy. The family was so poor that Vernon resorted to forging checks to pay the bills. He got caught and went to prison. "He only did it because we were hungry," Gladys cried when the police took him away. Elvis and his mother moved in with relatives, and money was tighter than ever. Music became Elvis's escape. He sneaked into "honky-tonk" bars to listen to black musicians play the blues. Back home, he sang and banged on a cardboard guitar he made himself. "Oh, honey, it could set your teeth to hurtin'!" is how an uncle described Elvis's first singing attempts.

For his eleventh birthday, Elvis begged his parents for a bike. They couldn't afford it, so they bought him a $7.95 guitar instead. With the new guitar, there was no stopping Elvis: he played for whoever would listen. In grade school, he sang in talent contests and wowed an audience of 200 at the state fair. He even sat outside a local radio station, singing along with the records, until the DJ invited him in. He was so impressed by Elvis's singing that he let the eleven-year-old perform on his show.

In 1948, the Presleys moved to Memphis, Tennessee in search of better work. Elvis had no friends and the kids saw him as a hick from the country who lived on the poor side of town. Throughout high school, he was quiet and kept to himself, rarely speaking in class. No one suspected the country boy had secret dreams of becoming a star.

> Elvis loved food. Once he wolfed down eight cheeseburgers, two BLT sandwiches, and three chocolate milkshakes—in one sitting! But his favorite food in the whole world was deep-fried peanut-butter and banana sandwiches! ❖

Even though he was a loner, Elvis stood out from the crowd. While the style for guys then was a natural-looking crew cut, Elvis had long hair which he dyed jet black and greased back. Popular guys played sports and wore preppy clothes. Not Elvis. A high school classmate remembers him:

Here was this classroom full of guys in jeans and T-shirts, penny loafers. . .and in the middle sat a dark-haired, dark-eyed boy in a pink sports coat, pink and black pants. . .He spilled out of his chair, legs spread forward and his arms hanging purposefully over the back of the chair. He had a look of disdain.

> Elvis, who would become one of the most infamous dancers in the world, didn't dance at his own prom. At the end of the night, he confessed to his disappointed date that he didn't know how. ❖

When a classmate told him, "You know, those clothes set you apart from everybody," Elvis grinned and said, "That's what I'm after."

After high school graduation, Elvis worked as a truck driver while trying to break into show biz. Less than a year after making his mother's birthday record, Elvis got his big break. Sun Records had a ballad to record, but no singer. They remembered the kid with the weird sideburns and decided to give him a shot. Nineteen-year-old Elvis couldn't believe it when they called and told him to be there in three hours. Twenty minutes later, the out-of-breath teen was at the studio. He had run all the way.

Elvis panicked when they didn't like his version of the ballad. But he blew them away when he belted out a song called "That's All Right (Mama)." They decided to record it instead. The song's mix of gospel, country, blues, and Elvis's unique voice created a totally new sound. Memphis radio stations ate it up. Phone calls poured into stations whenever it was played.

It wasn't long before word of Elvis spread beyond Memphis. As he traveled the South playing radio shows and concerts, he attracted more and more screaming fans. In 1955 RCA Records came calling: they agreed to pay Sun Records $40,000 to get the rising star, with a $5,000 bonus for Elvis. It was the highest amount ever paid for a pop singer, and more money than Elvis had ever seen. But RCA was really taking a gamble.

In 1950s America, adults listened to big band stars like Frank Sinatra and Doris Day. The music was nice, but definitely not radical. There was a new kind of music out there—*rock 'n' roll*—but it was performed mostly by black artists like Chuck Berry, Little Richard and Fats Domino. Most white Americans didn't know about rock 'n' roll because white radio stations refused to play black musicians. Teenagers were hungry for something new. . .something more dangerous. Elvis hit the scene at the perfect time. *Everything* about him was different and rebellious—his clothes, his hair, his music, and even his dancing. Musician Bob Dylan said, "Hearing him for the first time was like busting out of jail." Elvis was as controversial back then as Eminem is now, and parents hated him just as much.

Just after turning twenty-one, Elvis recorded his first single with RCA, "Heartbreak Hotel." Although most of the RCA executives hated the song and called it a sure "bomb," their gamble paid off. "Heartbreak Hotel" hit number one on the charts and sold over a million copies. Elvis was flooded with invitations to all the top TV shows. But it was America's number one program, *The Ed Sullivan Show*, that made him a star.

With 54 million people watching, the almost-famous singer strummed his guitar and growled, "I'm ready to rock and roll." The teenage studio audience went wild—guys stomped and howled while girls screamed and pulled their hair! But when the parents watching the show saw Elvis, with his long hair and bad-boy attitude, they really lost it. His dancing was so outrageous that the cameras would only show him from the waist up:

> *Spasms ran through both his legs, and soon the entire midsection of his body was jolting as if he'd swallowed a jackhammer.*

He was ridiculed as "Elvis the Pelvis" and "unspeakably vulgar."

Yet by the end of the show, host Ed Sullivan was won over by Elvis's polite Southern charm and told his millions of viewers, "This is a real decent, fine boy." Elvis was paid a record $50,000 for three appearances, but more important, Sullivan's comments helped calm parents and critics.

Just as his singing dreams were coming true, Elvis's other dream—to be a movie star—also took off. In 1956 he filmed his first movie, *Love Me Tender*. The movie and title song were hits, and Elvis was in heaven. Over the next ten years Elvis starred in dozens of movies—including *King Creole, G.I. Blues, Blue Hawaii,* and *Viva Las Vegas*—and while most of

Once in the middle of the night, Elvis flew a group of friends to Colorado in his private jet just to try his favorite Fool's Gold Sandwich: a full loaf of bread, stuffed with peanut butter, grape jelly and fried bacon! One sandwich, by itself, had 42,000 calories! ❖

them were silly musicals, they were popular and made piles of money.

After years of struggling in poverty, Elvis was a millionaire. And man, did he enjoy spending his money! He bought closets full of clothes and dozens of cars. But buying his Memphis mansion, Graceland, made him the happiest. His mother, father and grandmother moved in and filled the yard with eight ducks, two peacocks, one turkey, two pigs, and four donkeys!

After Elvis joined the army, enlistment went up by 25%! ❖

In 1958, at the height of his stardom, Elvis got drafted into the army. Most people expected him to get special treatment, like an easy job entertaining the troops, but Elvis wanted to be treated like everybody else. After years of being the outsider, he just wanted to be one of the guys. He even cut his famous hair into a crew cut. On the base in Germany, Elvis worked hard to earn the other soldiers' respect. His superior said, "I had ninety-six guys under my supervision, and none better than Presley."

While Elvis was in the army, in 1961, his mom Gladys died. Elvis, who was extremely close to his mother, was overcome with grief and guilt for being so far away during her last days. But it was during this time of grief that Elvis met his future wife: Priscilla Beaulieu, who was then the fourteen-year-old daughter of an army captain stationed in Germany. Elvis finished his army duty and in 1967, just after Priscilla turned twenty, they married. Their daughter, Lisa Marie, was born a year later.

Elvis decorated Graceland's 18 rooms just how he wanted. His "Jungle Room" had green carpet on the floor, walls and even the ceiling, an indoor waterfall, and furniture made out of animal horns! ❖

By the 1970s, Elvis's show biz life began to take its toll. Always on the road, always performing, his marriage fell apart. His high-fat diet led to a severe weight problem—he ballooned from a slim 160 pounds to over 300! And due to his non-stop touring and physically demanding shows, Elvis had problems falling asleep and chronic back pain. Doctors prescribed powerful sleeping pills and pain medication to keep him going. Soon Elvis was addicted. Although his friends and family worried about him, he refused to stop working. Elvis loved to perform and told them, "I hope I die on the stage." On August 16, 1977, at age forty-two, his body gave out, not on stage, but at home. He died and was buried at Graceland, next to his mother and twin brother. Tens of thousands of fans lined up for hours to pass by his grave and say goodbye.

The outsider from Tupelo lived his life to the fullest and got everything he ever dreamed of: fame, riches and respect. The shotgun shack where he was born is now a historic monument. Graceland sees almost a million visitors a year, second only to the White House, and the road that passes in front of it is now called Elvis Presley Boulevard.

Elvis poured his heart and soul into his songs, which are some of the most famous ever written—"Don't Be Cruel," "Hound Dog," "Blue Suede Shoes," "All Shook Up," "Jailhouse Rock," "Are You Lonesome Tonight?" He was the first to break down the barriers between black and white music and he changed it forever. Without Elvis, who knows, you might still be listening to be-bop instead of hip-hop. He was truly the King of Rock 'n' Roll.

I've always been a dreamer. My dreams have come true one hundred times over. –ELVIS PRESLEY

How Will You Rock the World?

My favorite way to rock the world would be to become a professional dancer. Studying dancing teaches you to stay focused and develop self-discipline. I'd like to be someone like Mikhail Baryshnikov or Rudolf Nureyev. I'd also like to educate people about dancing, and ballet in particular. Some people think that ballet is easy, or that it's only for girls. All dancers are athletes, but most people don't realize that.

Lucas Threefoot, age 12

Bruce Lee

1940 – 1973 ✦ *Martial Arts Expert/Actor* ✦
Hong Kong/United States

*Whenever I look around
I always learn one thing, and that is:
always be yourself. . .
express yourself, have faith in yourself.*

—BRUCE LEE

The night rain plastered Bruce Lee's hair to his head. He stood glaring at another twelve-year-old boy on the dark rooftop of his school. His fists were clenched tight as the other boy laughed and taunted him. A crowd began to gather and a few boys scrambled up the side of the building to catch a glimpse of the stand-off. The Chinese boys gathered behind Bruce and faced a growing gang of angry British boys.

"Hong Kong isn't yours," shouted one of the Chinese, and the two sides broke loose. Bruce dodged and ducked. He could see his friends fighting all around him—fists and feet were flying. He managed to land just one good punch before he got hit himself. As he blacked out, Bruce's last thought was, "I better learn how to defend myself."

This wasn't a scene from a famous Kung Fu movie. No, this was one of Bruce Lee's first real-life experiences with martial arts.

In San Francisco's Chinatown, a baby was born in the year of the dragon and the hour of the dragon—a double symbol of amazing luck and power to the Chinese. He was called Bruce Lee in English, but his Chinese name, *Jun Fan*, hinted at his future. It meant "to shake foreign countries."

Bruce and his parents moved back to Hong Kong when he was a baby and soon their apartment was crowded with four more children. It became even more crowded when

> Bruce had so much energy he couldn't keep still even while he was asleep. He often climbed down from his bunk bed and strolled around the apartment. . .sleepwalking!
> ❖

an aunt moved in with her five children, a maid, and assorted fish, cats and dogs! Bruce bounced from crowded room to room with such energy that his family nicknamed him *Mo Si Ting*, or "never sits still." The only thing that could keep the wild boy in one place was a good book, which he devoured in spite of his thick glasses.

Bruce's father was a performer in the famous Cantonese Opera, so Bruce grew up around actors. He was just three months old when he first appeared in a film! By age eighteen, Bruce had appeared in over twenty Chinese movies. Audiences called him "Little Dragon Lee," and loved him for his vivid expressions and intense emotion. But these small roles were nothing compared to the fame that would come later.

During Bruce's teen years, tensions were high in Hong Kong. The British had colonized the island, and many Chinese people were angry. They experienced plenty of racism from the colonizers and fights between British and Chinese boys were common. After twelve-year-old Bruce took a beating in a brawl, he decided to learn the martial arts.

In Hong Kong it was as common for boys to learn Kung Fu as it was for American boys to learn baseball. For five years, Bruce studied Kung Fu six hours a day, seven days a week. When he turned seventeen, he landed his first major role in *The Orphan*, a movie about a troubled kid. In the movie Bruce got to show off his fighting skills. It was a success, and soon he was offered more action roles. His mother, however, was against her son working in action-packed movies. Bruce had been in trouble at school for bad behavior and she was anxious about his fighting. After a lot of worrying, she sent him to the United States to live with friends. When Bruce took off for America, he was eighteen years old and had nothing but $100 in his pocket and butterflies in his stomach.

He moved in with his parents' friends in Seattle, Washington and worked at their restaurant as a busboy. Between work, Kung Fu practice, and high school, Bruce taught martial arts to his friends. When he started college at the University of Washington, he had so many students that he launched his own martial arts school.

> Believe it or not, the aim of Kung Fu is not to hurt other people, but to gain a sense of harmony and to end human conflict. ❖

Bruce had a different kind of fight on his hands when he fell in love. Linda Emery was white, and in the 1960s mixed-race relationships were not accepted. But Bruce and Linda were in love and got married anyway. Soon they had a baby boy named Brandon and moved to San Francisco, where Bruce opened another martial arts school.

> Bruce was lightning-fast. He once put a dime in a reporter's hand and told him to close his fist before he could grab the dime. The reporter closed his hand fast, but when he opened his fist the dime was gone. He had a penny instead! Bruce moved so fast the reporter didn't even see him. ❖

Bruce's Kung Fu reputation grew, and it wasn't long before Hollywood discovered him. While he won some roles, including the role of Kato, the Kung Fu fighting chauffeur on the TV series *The Green Hornet*, Bruce was frustrated with the racism he found in the show-biz industry. There were very few roles for Asian actors, and even roles that were written for Asians were often given to white actors instead.

His acting career stalled when he injured his back in 1970. Doctors told him he would never be able to do martial arts again, but Bruce ignored them and pushed himself to recover. While he was stuck in bed, he wrote his philosophy of fighting, which he called *Jeet Kune Do*. The philosophy covers both the physical techniques to Bruce's brand of Kung Fu and how to find inner harmony through the martial arts. It is now a best-selling book called *Tao of Jeet Kune Do.*

Discouraged by Hollywood's prejudice against Asians, Bruce returned to Hong Kong to make films. He was surprised to discover he was already a star there—*The Green Hornet* was a hugely popular TV show on the island. Fully recovered from his injury, Bruce made his first hit movie, *The Big Boss*, which became Hong Kong's top-selling movie. Next, he did *The Chinese Connection*, in which he played a martial arts instructor who fights against racist Japanese characters. The success of this movie made Bruce such a star and hero in China, that he was able to write, cast, direct and act in his next movie, *The Way of the Dragon.*

Now it was Hollywood's turn to come crawling back. American producers who told Bruce he was "too Asian" before were now begging him to star in their movies. He filmed just one American film, *Enter the Dragon,* but sadly never got to see it on the big screen. Just after filming, Bruce collapsed from a severe headache. Doctors told him it was caused by a mysterious swelling of his brain. He later took a pill to fix the headache and went to sleep. He never woke up. Bruce had no idea that he was allergic to the pill. It caused his brain to swell again and killed him. He died at age thirty-three, right at the peak of his career.

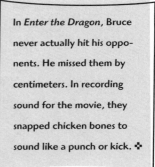

In *Enter the Dragon*, Bruce never actually hit his opponents. He missed them by centimeters. In recording sound for the movie, they snapped chicken bones to sound like a punch or kick. ❖

Enter the Dragon is still the most popular Kung Fu movie ever made. With his courage and talent, Bruce practically invented the Kung Fu movie, paved the way for minority actors in Hollywood, and opened doors for current action stars like Jackie Chan and Jean Claude Van Damme. With his creation of a new Kung Fu philosophy, *Jeet Kune Do*, Bruce also revolutionized how people thought about the martial arts. Bruce never let other people's prejudices stand in the way of his dreams. He opened the minds of audiences around the world and truly lived up to his name "to shake foreign countries."

Pelé

1940 – ✤ *Soccer Player* ✤ *Brazil*

If Pelé had not been born a man,
he would have been a ball.

–BRAZILIAN JOURNALIST

Dust was flying at the construction site, but it wasn't from jackhammers. . .a fierce soccer game was going on. Four grown men were huffing and puffing, sweat pouring down their faces as they tried to catch the small barefoot boy with the ball who was heading for their goal.

From the sidelines, a well-dressed man watched. One defender lunged towards the ball, but the boy flicked it over his foot and easily continued toward the goal. As he outran the other men, one tried an illegal slidetackle from behind. But it was as if the boy had eyes in the back of his head—just before the man slid into his heel, the boy dodged right and slammed the ball with his left foot into the space between two barrels. Goal! The observer, who was actually a scout for professional soccer teams, shook his head in amazement.

"Who's the kid?" he asked a worker.

"They call him Pelé."

That eleven-year-old boy would become the most famous, highest-paid athlete in the world, so beloved that fans would bow down before him, shouting "El Rey! El Rey!" (*the King*) when he entered the stadium.

Pelé was born in 1940 in a small Brazilian town, the son of a former soccer player. His full name was Edson Arantes do Nascimento. Because soccer is Brazil's national sport, most Brazilian boys dream of becoming soccer players. Pelé was no exception. But his family couldn't afford to buy him a ball, so his father stuffed an old sock full of rags and began teaching his son to play. By age five, Pelé ran wild in the streets, kicking his sock into makeshift goals.

School bored Pelé. He often played hooky and practiced soccer instead. By the fourth grade, Pelé had missed so much school he got kicked out. Fine with him. . .more time for soccer. He got a job as a cobbler (someone who fixes shoes), earning $2 a month. But more important, he was able to play soccer on his lunch break and after work with other workers in the neighborhood. The games were rough (no one called fouls) and played barefoot. Pelé loved it:

> *Often when I got home from my job and from the games we played I was very tired and would skip my dinner. But to me playing soccer was even more important than eating.*

Pelé so perfected one trick, it was named after him. The "Pelé Kick" looks like a back flip. Your foot meets the ball while you're airborne and your kicking leg is extended above your head, and the ball rockets back in the way it came—hopefully into the goal. Kids, don't try this at home! ❖

While in school, Pelé earned extra money shining shoes and selling peanuts outside movie theaters. ❖

Although Pelé was the youngest player, he was far better than the older guys. Gossip about the talented kid attracted Waldemar de Brito, one of Brazil's soccer stars and a recruiter for several teams. He watched

When rumors started that Santos was being offered a fortune to trade Pelé to another country's team, the Brazilian government actually declared Pelé a "national treasure," and therefore "non-exportable" to a foreign team. ❖

Pelé play one day at a construction site and was blown away: "I couldn't believe that such a young boy was able to perform some of the moves and tricks with the ball that Pelé was doing."

De Brito coached the boy for several years and when Pelé turned sixteen, de Brito decided he was ready for the big time: a try-out for a professional soccer team. As Pelé auditioned for the Santos soccer team, de Brito bragged to the coaches, "This boy will be the greatest soccer player in the world."

Pelé didn't let him down. While Pelé showed off his moves, the other players stopped practicing and stared in amazement. Santos signed him up that very day and in his first season, sixteen-year-old Pelé became the top scorer in the league—a title he held for years.

Though still young and inexperienced, Pelé's greatest wish was to represent his country in the 1958 World Cup. Few people thought he had a chance of making the national team since Brazil was a long shot to win and couldn't afford to take any chances. To everyone's surprise, Brazil took a chance. "I cried with joy when I got the news," Pelé said.

Pelé, which has no meaning, is a nickname his soccer buddies called him. He always hated it and prefered to be called Edson. ❖

Against the odds, Brazil fought its way into the finals, thanks to Pelé's constant scoring. In Brazil's final game against Sweden, Pelé had his back to Sweden's goal when he chest-trapped a pass. In an amazing gymnastic move, Pelé let the ball drop to his foot, chipped it over his shoulder, then flipped his body around and kicked the ball hard into the net before it could ever touch the ground! The Swedish goalie was so stunned, all he could do was cheer along with the thousands of ecstatic fans. "I've never seen anything like that before and I doubt if I ever will. . .again," the goalie said afterward. "It was unbelievable." Many people still claim Pelé's goal against Sweden was the most spectacular ever scored in the history of the World Cup. After the game, he was voted the top player in Brazil. At seventeen,

Pelé was a soccer legend.

He led his team to victory in two more World Cups (1962 and 1970), making Pelé the only person ever to win three World Cups. He also helped Santos win nine out of the next eleven national championships in Brazil. Before Pelé, people thought it was impossible for anyone to score 1000 goals. But during his 18-year career, Pelé did the impossible, scoring 1,220 goals, an average of one per game! That's like a baseball player hitting 70 home runs every year for 18 years.

Why, you might be wondering, was Pelé so incredible? Hard work was a big part of it. If Pelé felt he hadn't played his best, he would stay after a game and practice alone for hours. These thousands of hours of solitary practice helped him perfect his deadly-accurate kicks, increase his speed, and master countless tricks.

Brazilians take soccer very seriously. When they lost the 1966 World Cup, the country went into mourning: black flags hung from every window and many bridges were closed to prevent suicide attempts. ❖

Pelé did have a few secret weapons. It seemed to his fans that he must have ESP; he always seemed able to predict just what the other player was about to do. Pelé's ability was so unusual, Brazilian scientists actually studied him and found that his reaction time was a half-second faster than a normal human's, and his peripheral vision (the ability to see next to and behind you, while looking forward) was 25% stronger than the average Joe. This superhuman vision let Pelé pass to a teammate on the side while looking straight ahead, fooling his opponents.

Few soccer players, if any, are able to stay at the top of their game for more than five years. But Pelé played the world's best soccer for an incredible eighteen years! Today's soccer stars don't even dream of scoring 50 goals in a season. However, in Pelé's final season, he scored 52 goals. Since he had already scored over 100 goals in three different seasons, this measly 52 goals told him it was time to retire. He was already a multi-millionaire and had achieved his wildest boyhood dreams. He played again briefly from 1975 to 1977, when the New York Cosmos offered him $7 million to join

Pelé's experience as a cobbler came in handy for soccer. He often repaired his own soccer shoes, as well as those of his teammates. ❖

their team and promote soccer in the U.S. He led the team to the U.S. championship, then retired at 38, for good.

Pelé was the greatest soccer player the world has ever known, and some fans would argue he was the greatest athlete in history. His incredible talents brought soccer into the spotlight and introduced the world's most popular sport to the United States, where it thrives today. In 1980, international journalists named him Sportsman of the Century, and in 1994 Brazil appointed him its Minister of Sports. Although no longer playing soccer, Pelé stays active writing books, acting, composing music and managing his own international business empire.

As long as I can give some happiness I am happy. –PELÉ

How Will You Rock the World?

I am going to rock the world by becoming a famous athlete. To be precise, a NHL hockey star. I started skating lessons and hockey initiation when I was five and actually started real lessons when I was eight. I am now eleven and in the squirt level in hockey. I've got a long way to go to get to the NHL. I'm going to try hard to accomplish my dream to rock this world. I might get a scholarship.

Myles Schmertzler, age 11

Bob Dylan

1941 – ✤ *Singer/Songwriter* ✤ *United States*

Come mothers and fathers
Throughout the land
And don't criticize
What you can't understand
Your sons and your daughters
Are beyond your command
Your old road is
Rapidly agin'.
Please get out of the new one
If you can't lend your hand
For the times they are a-changin'

—BOB DYLAN, FROM "THE TIMES THEY ARE A-CHANGIN'"

he Golden Chords took their place backstage with the other talent-show hopefuls. The tap dancers, acrobats, and the girl with her accordion all looked the three young boys up and down with doubt. What were these scrawny thirteen-year-olds up to in their flashy gold jackets? Walking out on stage, the guys in the Golden Chords were nervous, but none more than Bob Zimmerman. He had recently developed a tic in his leg that acted up under stress. As the small audience clapped politely, Bob's leg began to thump the ground wildly. *Oh no*, he thought. But as they launched into their version of the Little Richard song "Jenny Jenny," the music possessed him. Bob cut loose, screaming and banging on the piano keys.

The band totally lost themselves in their song—their anxiety, and even the crowd, faded away. When they finished and snapped out of the zone, they fully expected screaming fans and a standing ovation. Instead, the crowd clapped politely again, smirks on their faces. Apparently Hibbing, Minnesota in 1957 was just not ready for Bob Zimmerman (later known as Bob Dylan) and his revolutionary rock and roll.

> Bob's first girlfriend was from the wrong side of the tracks, but he didn't care. They loved to dress up—she in leopard-skin tights and red lipstick, and he in a leather hat and pushed-up collar—and walk through downtown Hibbing, causing a stir. ❖

At Hibbing Junior High, anyone who was anyone played in the school band. Twelve-year-old Bob went out and bought himself a trumpet. He played and played for days, but couldn't make anything close to a pleasant noise come from the horn. So he traded the trumpet in for a saxophone. It was even worse. Bob returned that too. After trying two more failed instruments, Bob rented a cheap guitar. It changed his world. He experimented with the six strings for hours, until his fingers were raw. Eventually, the guitar became Bob's sidekick and confidante. He was rarely seen without it hanging across his shoulders.

In the 1950s, Hibbing was a conservative small town. There was only only one radio station, and it refused to play music "for the youth." Instead, it played what the housewives wanted to hear: polkas and songs by crooners like Frank Sinatra and Bing Crosby. On clear nights, Bob would walk for miles down the Mississippi River carrying his transistor radio, just to get reception from the big city rock-and-roll stations.

But the times, they were a-changin'. When Bob was sixteen, a new radio station popped up in Hibbing, and once a week it broadcast a DJ named Jim Dandy, whose show was wired in from Virginia. He played blues greats like Howlin' Wolf and Lightnin' Hopkins, two black performers whose music had never rocked the Hibbing airwaves before. Bob was such a fan of the show that he borrowed his father's car to make a pilgrimage to meet Jim Dandy.

When they finally met, Bob was amazed to find out that Jim "Dandy" Reese was a black man! Reese had slipped through the color lines of 1950s radio. He was an inspiration to Bob, who had been punished by his father for "singing black." For the next year, Bob went on several road trips to see his new friend. Reese introduced Bob to a whole new world of music. This was the world that would later inspire Bob to redefine the roots of folk music. As an adult, Bob often sang of the injustices done to blacks and other oppressed minorities in 1960s America.

After graduating from high school, Bob left Hibbing as fast as he could to go to college in Minneapolis. There he found kindred spirits. He hooked up with a growing group of political activists who hung out sipping coffee and playing "folk music" in a hip area called Dinkytown. In the late 1950s and early 60s, folk music was the voice of protest. The songs expressed young people's frustrations with injustice and with the government, which they saw as old, corrupt and useless. In Dinkytown Bob got his first taste of this powerful music and launched his new life as a folk singer by changing his name to Bob Dylan.

But Bob was too big, even for Dinkytown. He soon hit the road and found himself in New York City. In 1960, New York's Greenwich Village folk music scene was going crazy. Eighteen-year-old Bob was determined to become the greatest folk singer of all time and had his eye on the prize: a record deal with one of the big labels. He played tiny coffeehouses for $15 a day, sometimes playing till four in the morning.

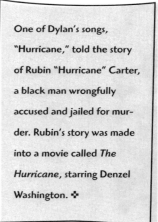

One of Dylan's songs, "Hurricane," told the story of Rubin "Hurricane" Carter, a black man wrongfully accused and jailed for murder. Rubin's story was made into a movie called *The Hurricane*, starring Denzel Washington. ❖

It wasn't until Bob began writing his own songs, that he finally hit the big-time. Up to that time, no one in folk music wrote original songs. It was sacrilege—like writing a new national anthem! But Bob had serious chutzpah. At his first big gig, opening for blues giant John Lee Hooker, Bob started out by singing two Woody Guthrie songs, and then he launched into his own (gasp!) original tune called "Song for Woody."

Some people were impressed, but many were horrified. When a glowing review came out in the *New York Times,* praising Bob's "genius," there was a big buzz heard on the street. Good or bad, Bob was changing the face of folk music and he wasn't even twenty years old! A few months later, Bob's dream came true—he signed a deal with Columbia Records.

His first album, *Bob Dylan,* was unlike anything on the radio at the time. Nowadays, angry protest songs are common. But back in the early 60s, most pop singers did love songs or light, fun, happy tunes. Not Bob. He wrote songs about the problems he was passionate about: war, racism, poverty. He wanted to shake people up. He wanted to change the world.

The album flopped, selling just a few hundred copies. Columbia prepared to drop Bob as soon as his contract was up, but his agent at Columbia, John Hammond, flew into a rage, telling the other executives that if they dropped him it would be "over his dead body." Since Hammond actually had a heart condition, Columbia took his threat seriously. They didn't want to lose one of their top executives, so they gave Bob a second chance.

Meanwhile, Bob madly wrote and rewrote. He was determined not to let poor sales get him down. Eventually, he came up with "Blowin' in the Wind," a social commentary that launched him to stardom.

How many times must a man look up
Before he can see the sky?
Yes, 'n' how many ears must one man have
Before he can hear people cry?
Yes, 'n' how many deaths will it take till he knows
That too many people have died?
The answer, my friend, is blowin' in the wind,
The answer is blowin' in the wind.

Bob finished the lyrics at a local coffee shop. A friend who was performing there heard Bob tinkering with it during a break and grabbed the lyrics from him. "Ladies and Gentlemen," he said from stage, "I'd like to sing a new song by one of our great songwriters. It's hot off the pencil, so here it goes." When he finished "Blowin' in the Wind," the entire crowd jumped to their feet and cheered. When the song was released on a later album, it became the first of many Bob Dylan hits.

Soon Bob was famous and his songs were being sung all across America and even around the world. But by age twenty-five, he was burnt out; the pressures of stardom were too much for him. He disappeared from the music scene for four years! The official story was that Bob had a motorcycle accident and was recovering. No one really knows if the story was true or an excuse to escape his crazy rock-star life.

Bob's son, Jakob Dylan, is the lead singer of the The Wallflowers (named for a tune Bob wrote in 1971). Jakob's popular song "Hand Me Down" is about growing up in the shadow of his famous father. ❖

True or not, the time out of the spotlight was good for Bob. He and his wife had two kids and fatherhood rejuvenated him, giving him a new sense of joy. Bob's disappearance didn't hurt his fame, either. In fact, he just got more popular! After all, he wasn't just a famous singer/songwriter, he was also *mysterious*. Bob made a triumphant return to the spotlight in 1968, to honor his idol Woody Guthrie at a memorial concert. After that, he played all kinds of different music, branching into electric guitar rock and roll, and returning to one of his first loves, the blues.

Bob Dylan's music is still played around the world, and he continues to record and perform today. As a boy he dreamed of making a difference through his music. His songs of protest have made such a difference that Bob has been nominated for the Nobel Prize in Literature three times. The Nobel committee praised him:

> *His blend of poetry and social consciousness with music is entirely appropriate for Nobel recognition. His songs…have been passionately concerned with civil rights, world peace, the preservation of the environment, and other crucial global causes.*

Bob Dylan's music still inspires passion, frustration, beauty and change in listeners, reminding us all to make our own difference in the world.

Chico Mendes

1944 - 1988 ✤ *Environmental Human Rights Activist* ✤ *Brazil*

Chico Mendes was a butterfly flapping his wings over the forest. He started a storm that is still rising above the Amazon, a storm that may yet break across the world.

–DR. STEPHAN SCHWARTZMAN, ANTHROPOLOGIST WITH ENVIRONMENTAL DEFENSE

The enormous crash of a falling tree shook the ground as they walked. Chico yelled to the group of fifty following him, "Don't worry, friends, we'll be okay. But please watch out for falling branches." The buzzing of chainsaws grew louder as they made their way through the thick rainforest. The people following Chico were mostly rubber tappers who lived and depended on this land that had been taken from them and was now being destroyed.

As they approached the clear-cut site, the sound of chainsaws was deafening. They could see what looked like a cemetery, the charred, blackened tree stumps jutting out from the barren earth. They could also see a man with a gun guarding the area. His orders were to shoot anyone who tried to stop the cutting. Chico's unarmed group kept walking toward the destruction, hoping they looked braver than they felt. They stuck close together, the women squeezing their children's hands to give them courage.

25% of the drugs we use in the western world contain rainforest products, yet only 1% of rainforest plants have been studied for their medical uses. ❖

"Please stop!" a marcher yelled over the noise. The guard and the loggers turned and stared in amazement. *What were women and children doing here?* Pointing his gun at the group, the guard ordered them to leave. They didn't move. Tension hung in the air as the minutes ticked by and everyone waited to see what would happen. Finally, the guard dropped his gun. He didn't care if his boss fired him, he couldn't shoot women and children. The loggers shut off their giant saws and walked out into the jungle. The cutting was over.

Chico Mendes led many of these peaceful protests, called *empates*. He inspired the people who lived and worked in the jungles of Brazil to rise up and fight for their land and their way of life and his courage led the way for the environmentalists who followed in his footsteps.

The Brazilian rainforest, where Chico grew up, is the largest tropical rainforest left on earth. At 1.2 billion acres, it is equal in size to the ninth largest country in the world. The "rainforest" gets its name from the abundant rain that falls there. Even in the dry season, rain falls every day. All that rain has helped to create an environment that has more species of plants and animals per square foot than anywhere else on earth. The incredible number of trees in the rainforest breathe in carbon dioxide (a gas pollution that cars and other man-made machines give off) and turn it back into oxygen, which helps keep the earth's ozone layer intact.

One kind of rubber tree has exploding fruit! The fruit flings its seeds more than fifty feet. ❖

It is easy to imagine why Chico was so protective of this place. He was born in northwestern Brazil in 1944, and spent his days playing beneath trees as tall as skyscrapers and chasing butterflies bigger than his head. But Chico's parents were rubber tappers, and for them, life in the jungle could be very hard. They got up before sunrise and worked long into the evening.

By age nine, Chico was tapping rubber too. He walked twenty miles a day, tapping 150-200 trees. He carefully cut V-shaped lines into each rubber tree's trunk and let the white sap run out into a tin cup he set below (back then people used this sap to make rubber for tires). During these long walks, Chico grew to appreciate the rainforest and to understand that each part is there for a reason; the animals, trees and even the insects play an important role in maintaining the intricate web of life.

> You'd have a hard time breathing without the Amazon rainforest. It is called the "lungs of our planet" because it constantly recycles carbon dioxide (what we breathe out) into oxygen (what we breathe in). It produces more than 20% of the world's oxygen! ❖

Wealthy men called "rubber barons" ran the rubber plantations, but the workers were mostly Amazon Indians and other poor people lured into rubber tapping by the promise of a good life. But the good life never came. The bosses kept workers in debt by paying them next to nothing and overcharging them for food and lodging. For all their long hours, workers usually owed the bosses more money than they earned. They could never get out of debt or save enough to leave, so they became like slaves.

Even if they could leave, most had nowhere else to go. They couldn't read and had no other job skills. The rubber barons didn't want workers learning how to read—if workers were educated, they might figure out how they were being cheated. Chico's father, however, could read a little and each night, after a long day of work, he taught his son how. When Chico was twelve, a Brazilian journalist named Euclides Tavora visited the Mendes house and was impressed by the boy's reading skills. He offered to teach Chico, who happily began spending weekends at Tavora's book-filled house.

> 50% to 90% of all life forms exist in the rainforest! ❖

When Chico was twenty, he started teaching other workers how to read when he wasn't tapping rubber trees. He knew the rubber barons were corrupt and that workers had to get educated if they wanted to fight back. Five years later, he quit rubber tapping to teach full-time and also began organizing worker protests.

When a man-made rubber was created in the 1970s, demand for Brazil's natural rubber went down the tubes. The rubber barons had to find another way to make money, so they switched to cattle ranching. They began cutting and burning down millions of acres of rainforest to create land for their cows to graze on. When a chunk of forest the size of California was burned down, forcing all the people who lived there to leave their homes, Chico knew it was time for drastic action.

He started up the National Council of Rubber Tappers and promoted nonviolent demonstrations. Chico spent years battling the stubborn Brazilian government, trying to get them to protect large portions of the Amazon rainforest where rubber tappers could live. But the ranchers had the government in their pockets. They hardly protected any land at all and acted like Chico and the rubber tappers didn't exist.

> The Amazon river flows for thousands of miles through the Brazilian rainforest, and holds more types of fish than the entire Atlantic Ocean! ❖

In 1987, Chico was invited to the United States by environmentalists concerned about the destruction of the rainforest. He explained how rubber tappers lived without harming the land and asked for their help in convincing the Brazilian government to stop further destruction of the land. By then, an area twice the size of California had been destroyed. Burning all that land was causing huge problems. When fires burn, they give off carbon dioxide, a gas that traps heat to the earth's surface. When too much carbon dioxide is released, the planet begins to warm up, causing the ecosystems of plants and animals to suffer. This is called the "greenhouse effect."

Chico received two awards for his efforts, one from the United Nations Environmental Program and a medal from the Better World Society. But when he returned to Brazil after the conferences, the ranchers were extremely angry that Chico had brought world attention to their actions. As the ranchers got angrier, Chico resolved to make more progress. He led more and more empates, and succeeded in saving more than 20,000 acres from being burned in 1988 alone.

But just when he was starting to turn things around in Brazil, Chico was shot and killed by a group of ranchers on December 22, 1988. Everyone knew who were responsible for Chico's death, but were too afraid of them to speak up.

Chico's death made headlines all over the world, and brought even more attention to the environmental damage the ranchers were doing to

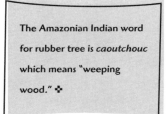

The Amazonian Indian word for rubber tree is *caoutchouc* which means "weeping wood." ❖

the rainforest. In 1989, several U.S. senators flew to Brazil to talk about environmental programs. Under pressure from the media, the Brazilian government approved a plan to replant 2.5 million acres of deforested land. They also stopped logging in much of the rainforest that Chico had fought for, instead creating nature reserves. They called first 2.4 million acre reserve the "Chico Mendes Extractive Reserve."

In 1992, leaders from all over the world met in Brazil for the United Nations Conference on the Environment. Unfortunately, Chico couldn't be there, but all remembered him as the greatest champion and defender of the rainforest. Chico fought his whole life to preserve the land that he loved, and his memory inspires people all over the world to continue in the fight to save the still rapidly disappearing rainforest.

How Will You Rock the World?

I will rock the world by becoming an architect. I will design bigger, better and definitely safer buildings. I will design them to help the environment so that they don't pollute the air as much as other buildings do. I also want to be the first person to design underwater living environments so that there won't be as many people crammed onto one continent. I will also design buildings for people who are less fortunate and I will do my best to listen to other people's ideas when designing new buildings.

Kevin Walker, age 11

Stephen King

1947– ✤ United States ✤ Writer

"King paints a masterful, terrifying picture of every child's (and maybe adult's) worst fear."

—*ST. LOUIS DISPATCH*

The high-school sophomore handed out copies of his latest writing effort, *The Village Vomit*, to classmates and friends. Similar to *MAD* magazine, Stephen's pseudo-newspaper made fun of everyone at Lisbon Falls High School, from jocks to teachers, cheerleaders to nerds. Stephen thought his stories were hilarious—but would the other kids like it?

He had no need to worry. Filled with "news" items like farting cow contests and faculty characters like Miss Rat Pack and Miss Maggot (real-life teachers Miss RayPach and Miss Margitan)—the *Vomit* was a hit! It wasn't long before everyone in school was reading Stephen's 'zine and "busting a gut," as he described it. Though most of the teachers could take a joke, Miss "Maggot" was not pleased. Issues of *The Vomit* were confiscated and destroyed. Stephen was sent to detention!

Luckily, the principle appreciated Stephen's writing abilities more than his sense of humor. Instead of giving him detention, he arranged for Stephen to write for a real paper, the *Weekly Enterprise*, covering high-school sports. Stephen, who played high school football, was perfect for the job. He quickly learned the ins and outs of professional writing, and was happy to earn a penny for each word he wrote. In the future, Stephen King would earn a *lot* more for his writing—in fact his stories would make him a household name and a millionaire many times over!

Born on September 21, 1947 in the coastal town of Portland, Maine, Stephen King was considered a miracle baby. Doctors told Stephen's mother Ruth that she would never be able to give birth, so the baby was an unexpected arrival. When Stephen was two, his father left and it was up to his mother to support the family single-handedly. Over the next ten years, they moved a lot—Indiana, Connecticut, Wisconsin. . .wherever Ruth could find a job. Eventually, they ended up in Durham, Maine, where Ruth cared for Stephen's grandparents. They moved into a two-story farmhouse with no running water. This was the 1950s, but they had to carry all their drinking water in from a well. There wasn't even a bathroom—they had to use an outhouse instead!

Durham was tiny, with not much going on. Bored and isolated at the farmhouse, Stephen quickly developed a love for comic books. An avid reader herself, Ruth encouraged him to read and write, giving Stephen a quarter for each story he created. When he was only seven, Stephen wrote his first "scary" story about a dinosaur taking over a small town. He was particularly drawn to horror comic books, science fiction, and fantasy novels, like *Lord of the Rings*.

Although he was not the most popular boy, by middle school Stephen was becoming famous for his stories. He wrote one about some students

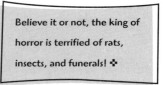

Because Durham was so small, there was no school bus and Stephen had to ride in a taxi to high school. But it was no ordinary taxi—it was a converted hearse! ❖

Believe it or not, the king of horror is terrified of rats, insects, and funerals! ❖

taking over their school and handed out chapters to his classmates as he finished them. They waited on pins and needles, wishing Stephen could write faster. You see, all the characters in the suspenseful story were based on the real kids in his school—and they couldn't wait to find out what they would do next in Stephen's story!

In high school, Stephen was an offensive tackle for the football team and played guitar in a rock band called the MoonSpinners. Though Stephen had other interests in high school, but he was still obsessed with writing. He and his best friend Chris Chelsey made a book of their horror stories, including doozies by Stephen like "The Cursed Expedition" and "The Thing at the Bottom of the Well." Using a beat-up mimeograph machine, they made copies of their collection, *People, Places and Things— Volume 1*, to sell. The book's introduction read:

> *We warn you. . .the next time you lie in bed and hear an*
> *unreasonable creak or thump, you can try to explain it away*
> *. . .but try Steve King's and Chris Chelsey's explanation:*
> People, Places and Things.

Before graduating, Stephen not only completed his first novel, *The Aftermath*, but also began sending his writing to publishers. One of his short stories, "I Was A Teenage Graveyard Robber," got published and he also won a magazine essay contest.

Stephen went to the University of Maine, where he was active in student politics and protested the Vietnam War. There he contin-

Stephen King is the world's best-selling novelist. ❖

ued writing and even had a weekly column in the college newspaper called "King's Garbage Truck," named for the grab bag of topics he covered. The column gave Stephen a lot of freedom—he wrote about movies, books, politics. . .whatever struck his fancy. He also sold his first story. *Starling Mystery Stories* paid him $35 for "The Glass Floor." It wasn't much, but Stephen was psyched to be making money from his writing!

But making a *living* as a writer wasn't so easy. After college, Stephen got married and had a daughter, and with a family to support he took a job at a Laundromat. Fortunately, after a year of washing clothes, Stephen got a job he liked more: teaching high school English. He still found time to write every day, hoping his stories might sell and help pay the bills. He sent his novel *The Running Man* to dozens of publishers who all rejected it (years later it was made into a movie starring Arnold Schwarzenegger and Sharon Stone). But one editor at Doubleday Publishing thought Stephen had potential, and told him to keep sending stories.

When Stephen meets with his editors, he likes to do it over hot dogs and peanuts at Yankee Stadium. ❖

Stephen almost didn't. The next book he wrote was *Carrie*, the story of an unpopular girl who uses her telepathic powers to get revenge on teasing classmates. Stephen hated it so much he threw it in the garbage! Luckily, his wife fished it out and convinced him to send it to Doubleday. They loved it. Stephen almost passed out when he got their telegram: "'Carrie' officially a Doubleday book, $2,500 advance against royalties, congrats, kid—the future lies ahead." The money came just in time—Stephen was broke, he couldn't even afford a phone.

He was elated to see his first novel published (and to get a phone!), but $2,500 was still not enough money to quit his day job. Then, in 1973 Doubleday sold the paperback rights for *Carrie* to another company and Stephen got another surprise. He would get $200,000 for the sale!

Stephen got the idea for his book *Pet Semetary* when his cat Smucky got killed by a car. ❖

Carrie went on to become one of Stephen's most popular novels, and in 1976, a movie was released, starring Sissy Spacek and John Travolta. According to Stephen, "The movie made the book and the book made me." Stephen could finally afford to leave his job teaching and write full time.

Over the next decades, Steven wrote some of the best-selling and scariest stories of all time: *Salem's Lot, Cujo, IT, Pet Semetary, The Shining,* and *The Stand*. After the popularity of *Carrie*, each book earned Stephen millions. Instead of the trailer they had once called home, the Kings moved into a 123-year-old mansion, complete with 23 rooms and a black iron fence decorated with bats and spiderwebs. The house is even rumored to be haunted by the ghost of an old general!

Over 100 million copies of Stephen's books are now in print and can be read in 32 different languages. Many of his stories have been made into movies: *Carrie, The Shining, Stand By Me, The Shawshank Redemption,* and *The Green Mile,* to name a few. Just like his high-school classmates, now millions of fans are spellbound by Stephen's tales. But for Stephen King, writing has always been his life's passion, ever since he wrote his first stories for his mom, at a quarter apiece.

How Will You Rock the World?

I'm going to rock the world by becoming a children's book writer. I will write picture books, chapter books and history books. I have a special book that I write poems in whenever I can. I've written a poem called "The Living Desert" and a story called, "Kevin, the Duck." My poem, "Ducky is Lucky" is published in the July 2000 issue of Kidshighway magazine in Texas.

Jure Erlic, age 8

Matt Groening

1954 – ✤ *Cartoonist* ✤ *United States*

Most grown-ups forget
what it was like to be a kid.
I vowed I would never forget.

–MATT GROENING

In the back row of the class, Bart Simpson sits hunched over his desk, scribbling a drawing of his dog, Santa's Little Helper, in the margins of his notebook. Mrs. Krabappel walks the aisles menacingly.

"Today class, I am handing back your multiplication tests. *Most* of you passed. *Some* of you however…" she says, whipping her head around to stare directly at Bart. She is not smiling.

"Baaart," she barks, "I don't recall assigning *pet portraits* for last night's homework. Quit it, Michelangelo!"

"Chill out, man," says Bart, continuing his masterpiece. Mrs. Krabappel sighs and sends him to Principal Skinner's office. . .again.

This could be a scene from *The Simpsons*. But it's not. With a few name changes, this was the real-life childhood of Matt Groening (pronounced like "raining"), future creator of that hugely popular animated TV show. Sure, he's famous and well-respected now, but back then he was just another kid getting into trouble. A lot.

> The streets of Portland, Oregon scream *The Simpsons*. There's Flanders St. (Ned Flanders), Lovejoy St. (Reverend Lovejoy), Terwilliger Blvd. (Bob Terwilliger, aka Sideshow Bob), and Quimby St. (Mayor Quimby). ❖

The Simpsons was inspired by Matt's tortured childhood, which he spent in Portland, Oregon. His dad was a cartoonist and encouraged his son's early doodling habit. Matt doodled his way into high school, drawing cartoons in every class, even P. E.! He even remembers "injuring himself severely while doodling on the parallel bars." Although Matt's constant cartooning got him into trouble at school, he finally found an outlet for all that energy scribbling around inside him. At fourteen, he started drawing a cartoon strip for his high school newspaper. But just like Bart, Matt's wacky sense of humor got him into trouble and he eventually got kicked off the newspaper staff. Bet they're sorry now!

After high school, Matt went to Evergreen College in Olympia, Washington. It's hard to say whether he chose the school because of their great art department or because they don't give grades. At the time, Matt considered himself more of a writer—he actually thought that he was a lousy cartoonist and that all his friends could draw better than he could. But one friend, fellow cartoonist Lynda Barry (creator of the popular illustrated character *Marlys*), never let him give up on his art, even when he wanted to quit. Matt kept on doodling, and eventually got better and better. His simple style is now copied by cartoonists everywhere.

> If you switch the letters around, B-A-R-T actually spells B-R-A-T. Spooky. ❖

In 1977, after college, Matt packed up and moved to Los Angeles hoping to become a writer. Just as he pulled into town at 2 A.M., his car broke down in the fast lane of the Hollywood Freeway. This nightmarish experience inspired another cartoon strip, "Life in Hell." Instead of sending his friends back in Oregon grouchy letters complaining about L.A., he sent them cartoon strips about how sorry his life was. His main character Binky, who always moped and complained about how unfair life is, was a rabbit because it was the easiest thing for Matt to draw. When some editors at the newspaper Matt worked for, the *Los Angeles Reader,* got a look at his strip one day, they thought "Life in Hell" was hilarious. They began running it in the paper and Matt developed a huge following. Soon you could see "Life in Hell" in 250 newspapers around the world.

In 1985, a TV producer saw "Life in Hell" and asked Matt to draw an animated short for a new comedy show called *The Tracy Ullman Show.* Legend has it that just fifteen minutes before a meeting with the big TV executives, Matt was informed that he should show them something new and original. While in the waiting room, he frantically sketched a family of characters, giving them the names of his own family: Homer, Marge, Lisa, Maggie. The only name he changed was his—Matt became Bart. In the meeting, the bigwigs asked what Homer did for a living and Matt blurted out the first thing that popped into his head: "He works in a nuclear plant." They cracked up, and *The Simpsons* was born.

The original shorts were just two minutes long and the characters looked quite different from the Simpsons we know today: Bart had lots more spikes on his head, Marge's hair was taller, Lisa just looked silly, and Homer didn't say "D'oh" even once.

Audiences weren't crazy about *The Tracy Ullman Show,* but they loved the Simpson family, so Fox gave them their own 30-minute TV show in 1989.

When you take a look at almost any hilarious *Simpsons* script, it's easy to see why Matt considered himself a writer instead of a cartoonist:

From the episode "Bart Gets Famous"

Setting: a factory tour

Bart: Have any of the workers ever had their hands cut off by the machinery?

Guide: No—

Bart: And then the hand started crawling around and tried to strangle everybody?

Guide: No, that has never happened.

Bart: Any popped eyeballs?

Guide: I'm not sure what kind of factory you're thinking of; we just make boxes here.

> The voices of Mr. Burns, Smithers, Ned Flanders, Principal Skinner, Otto, Reverend Lovejoy, Kent Brockman, and many more are all done by one man: Harry Shearer! Hank Azaria does Apu, Moe, and Chief Wiggum, among others. ❖

The Simpsons went down in history as the very first animated show to get a prime-time slot. Fox executives took a chance when they decided to do *The Simpsons* not as an after-school cartoon for kids, but as an evening show for both kids *and* adults. Their gamble paid off. Even though the show has been accused of being obnoxious and offensive, you can bet almost everyone will laugh at Bart's chalkboard messages that start each episode: "I will not trade pants with others," or maybe, "Beans are neither musical nor fruit." Yes, it is rude and crude, but it also makes you laugh until your stomach hurts. With reruns, it is doubtful the show will ever stop, until *The*

> Bart's voice is done by a girl! Nancy Cartwright has been doing Bart, Nelson, Todd Flanders, and Ralph Wiggum since the show began. ❖

Simpsons achieves world domination and Bart becomes ruler of the land. And there will be Matt, wringing his hands and laughing maniacally, just like Mr. Burns.

Bill Gates

1955– ✤ Business Tycoon ✤ United States

"Software creation is a mix of artistry and science."

—*BILL GATES*

Sixteen-year-old Bill looked up from the Traf-O-Data—a machine he and his friend Paul invented to solve traffic problems. The city official sat on the couch in the Gates' living room and cleared his throat, waiting impatiently for Bill's demonstration to start. Bill fed a piece of tape with instructions into the Traf-O-Data, which was designed to analyze cumbersome traffic data in a matter of minutes. The machine whirred a few times, then nothing.

"Tell him, Mom. Tell him it *really* works!"

"I don't have time for this, kid," the man said in frustration, getting up to leave. "Try me again when you're out of high school."

Little did the city official know that this frustrated boy standing before him would become the youngest billionaire in U.S. history. But Bill knew. He had already told many of his friends that he would be a millionaire by age twenty-five. Even at sixteen, he had already founded his own computer company and invented the Traf-O-Data machine.

William Henry Gates III (or Trey, as his family called him) was born in Seattle in 1955. His parents were strict and enforced several house rules: keep your room clean and no TV on weeknights. Without TV, Bill devoured countless books—especially science fiction. But no matter how much his parents bugged him, Bill's room was a disaster area. This messy look would later become one of his trademarks at Microsoft.

> Computer "bugs" first got their name in 1945 when a research assistant found a moth in one of the first experimental computers. ❖

The Gates family played lots of board games together, and Bill was extremely competitive. In fact, he was competitive in just about *everything*. When Bill's teacher assigned the class to write four to five pages, Bill wrote thirty. But his enthusiasm didn't help his grades much, so Bill's parents transferred him to a private school in the seventh grade. He struggled academically and socially during his first year at the new school. He was much smaller than other boys his age and he had enormous feet—size 13—but eventually he made some friends, including Kent Evans. Bill and Kent both liked math and science, and read *Fortune* magazine together. "We were going to conquer the world," said Bill.

After two years at the private school, Bill found his niche. That year the school bought a Teletype machine. At the time, the only computers in existence were huge mainframe computers that cost millions of dollars. The Teletype machine connected the school to a mainframe computer downtown and the students were charged an hourly rate for their computer time. Bill hung out in the computer room constantly and soon learned the programming language BASIC (Beginner's All-purpose Symbolic Instruction Code) to communicate with the computer. He created his first computer program, a tic-tac-toe game, at thirteen! He then wrote other game programs: a lunar landing game and computer versions of his favorite board games, *Risk* and *Monopoly*.

Bill was addicted to the computer and soon met other computer nerds, including Paul Allen. By ninth grade, Bill's grades were vastly improved. "I came up with a new form of rebellion," he said. The computer offered an outlet for Bill's creative and mathematical mind but it also got him into trouble. Some of his programs were known to crash the entire mainframe. Bill and his friends often broke into the computer's security system to change their computer time so they would be charged less. When the hackers were eventually caught, Bill was almost expelled!

In 1985, Bill and Paul Allen donated $2.2 million to their old high school for a math and science center named after Kent Evans. ❖

As his reputation for programming grew, Bill was often approached by teachers asking for computer help. The school wanted Bill and Kent to design a computer program to help with class scheduling. They even offered to pay them for it! But a week later, tragedy struck. Kent, who had gone mountain climbing, fell and died. Bill was devastated by his best friend's death; they had been inseparable since they had first met. For weeks Bill was stunned, incapable of doing anything at all. He eventually went back to work on the scheduling program, asking Paul Allen to help him finish.

Bill and Paul went on to create the Traf-O-Data machine. Even though Traf-O-Data didn't *always* work perfectly, it was a success. Cities all over the Northwest and Canada eventually used it to analyze traffic data and reduce congestion on city streets. As the money began to flow in, Bill's business skills emerged. He hired his buddies and classmates to work for the company. From their invention, Bill and Paul earned over $20,000 (which in 1970 was a serious chunk of change for a couple of teenagers!). They also helped design a computer program for the Bonneville Power Administration to control the power grid for the entire Northwest and a program for TRW, a defense contractor.

Bill and his wife Melinda have made some of the largest charity donations in history. They have donated $5 billion to the William H. Gates Foundation and $1.3 billion to the Gates Learning Foundation. ❖

With his improved grades and high test scores, Bill won a National Merit Scholarship and was accepted at Harvard, where he studied literature, social science, math, and chemistry. But his mind was always on computers. People thought Bill was crazy when he predicted that, one day, everyone would have *their own personal computer*.

As a break from work, Bill and his friends would sometimes sneak onto empty construction sites and have bulldozer races! ❖

Bill's prediction was on track when, in 1975, Ed Roberts invented the Altair. Although the Altair couldn't do much compared to today's computers (it had only 4K of memory and didn't even have a keyboard) it *was* the first PC. A technical revolution had arrived—and Bill and Paul hoped to be a part of it. They formed a new company called Microsoft (an abbreviation for microcomputer software) and decided to build a BASIC software program for the Altair. For the next seven weeks, Bill and Paul worked day and night to create the program. Finally, they finished it—the *first* software program for a PC. Bill was just nineteen years old.

Orders began pouring in for their new computer software—the first year revenues were more than $100,000! By January of 1977, Bill dropped out of Harvard to run Microsoft full time. He and Paul hired some of their old computer pals from Lakeside to work for them. Known as the Microkids, this gang of computer programmers were anything but typical. Many customers were shocked to hear rock music playing as the long-haired Microkids created software in jeans and T-shirts, instead of the suits and ties typical of most businesses.

Bill used some of his fortune to build his dream house. It has a theater, a dining room that seats 120 people, a trampoline room, a swimming pool, and parking space for his twenty sports cars. ❖

In 1981, Bill met with IBM to discuss the opportunity of a lifetime. IBM wanted Microsoft to develop an operating system for its new PC. Even though Bill was late for the meeting (he had to buy a tie first) he convinced IBM to go with Microsoft. IBM's new PC became a hit, and every IBM computer had Microsoft software. At twenty-four, Bill had made the deal of the century! Other computer companies began making IBM "clones" (copies of IBM's PC), and they *all* used Microsoft software.

By 1987, thirty-two-year-old Bill Gates was the youngest billionaire in the country. Today, Microsoft is a multibillion-dollar company whose software can be found on more than 75 percent of all computers.

Because of Microsoft's success, it has also received some negative attention. Owners of other computer companies have accused Microsoft of stealing their ideas and of using monopoly power to put them out of business. In July 2000, the federal government determined that Microsoft acted like a monopoly and should be broken up into smaller companies. Whether or not Microsoft gets broken up, Bill Gates has left his thumbprint on the history of information technology and will continue doing what he loves most—inventing the software of the future.

How Will You Rock the World?

I will rock the world be being an engineer that designs computers, because I know a lot about computers and have experienced putting a computer

together with my dad. I'm also very good at math and figuring things out—like problem solving and coming up with creative solutions.

Jeffrey Allen Haskell, age 11

Cameron Crowe

1 9 5 7 - ✤ Journalist/Movie Director ✤
United States

Love the job. Be the job.

—CAMERON CROWE

The fifteen-year-old kid shifted his weight from foot to foot, his breath forming puffs of mist in the air. He had been waiting for twenty minutes in the freezing cold for the band to arrive at the backstage door. He clutched a small yellow pad and his favorite pen. Finally, a big silver bus pulled up and four guys in big furry coats and sunglasses stepped off. As they pushed past the crowd of excited fans, he stuck out his pad of paper toward one of the band members.

"Excuse me," he said, "I'm here to…" But the rocker interrupted him by snatching his pad and scribbling a flamboyant signature across the entire page. The kid looked down at his pad, then back up at the backs of the band members as they disappeared into the backstage door.

"Wait. . .I'm here to interview you for *Rolling Stone* magazine," he shouted, "not to get an autograph." His voice trailed off as the door slammed shut.

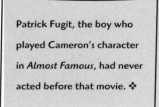

Cameron is married to a real-life rocker, Nancy Wilson of the band Heart. ❖

Cameron Crowe did eventually get his interview, but it took a lot of convincing for the security guard to let him in, and then even more convincing for the group to let a fifteen-year-old interview them. At that time, a bad review could break a band, and most rock stars were amazed to discover that a kid wielded such power over their careers. It *was* hard to believe that a teenager was writing for premier rock magazine *Rolling Stone*. But it was true, and Cameron would soon become well known, not only as a gifted writer, but also as a trustworthy friend to the bands.

Amazingly, this rock 'n' roll scribe was forbidden to listen to that kind of music when he was a kid. His mother, a college professor, believed it was "filth disguised as candy." It was Cameron's sister who first introduced him to rock 'n' roll. When she left for college, she gave him all her forbidden records. Crowe locked himself in his room for hours, secretly poring over such gems as *Led Zeppelin II, Deep Purple*, and the Beach Boys' *Pet Sounds*

Cameron quickly fell in love with rock music and searched out anything having to do with it. In the early 1970s, you had to be eighteen to buy rock magazines like *Creem* or *Rolling Stone*, but Cameron made

Patrick Fugit, the boy who played Cameron's character in *Almost Famous*, had never acted before that movie. ❖

friends with the man at the shop where they were sold, and he let Cameron look at them while hanging out in the shop.

Cameron's fate as an extraordinary teen was sealed when his sister took him to a meeting for the local alternative paper, the *San Diego Door*. At the meeting, he talked to lots of cool people who encouraged him to get into journalism. But when the fourteen-year-old asked if he could write music reviews for the journal, the staff was unsure. They believed rock and roll was a money making scam. But eventually they gave in and put Cameron in touch with

Lester Bangs, a former *Creem* and *Rolling Stone* writer. Cameron was so excited he could barely stand it; Bangs was a professional rock journalist!

Bangs gave Cameron lots of advice, and the next year he was ready to submit his own writing to *Rolling Stone*. He lied about his age, telling them he was eighteen. The editor there was truly impressed with Cameron's writing and hired him to interview Richie Furay of the band Poco (other band members included such greats as Neil Young and Stephen Stills, who would later form Crosby, Stills, Nash and Young). Cameron did such a great job with the interview that in 1973 *Rolling Stone* made him a permanent staff writer. He was just sixteen years old.

Cameron's first traveling assignment was a tour with the Allman Brothers. His mother freaked out a bit, but then realized it was Cameron's opportunity of a lifetime. The band was notorious for giving short and guarded interviews. And they didn't trust *Rolling Stone*, which had published some harsh reviews of their music. But Cameron had a strange effect on rock stars; he was so young and sincere that bands opened up to him, telling him all sorts of secrets they would never tell other reporters.

> The first film Cameron directed was one he also wrote. 1989's *Say Anything* starred John Cusack and was about a dorky outsider who falls for a brainy, popular girl. ❖

In his years as a journalist, Cameron interviewed such rock legends as Led Zeppelin, the Allman Brothers, Yes, The Who, David Bowie, Elton John, Peter Frampton, Lynyrd Skynyrd and most everyone else you hear on classic rock stations. Cameron made a name for himself writing catchy, true-to-life articles and for never betraying a band's trust. And they all loved him for it. Many bands refused to be interviewed by anyone else because Cameron was the only writer they liked.

By 1979, the twenty-two-year-old writer had big plans for a book. Although Cameron never finished high school, he decided to go undercover in a southern California high school in order to get inside the mind of the American teen. He enrolled in classes, pretending to be a senior named Dave Cameron, and immediately blended right in. No one suspected a thing. He hung out with his new friends after school and at the mall, he went to their parties and to football games. When something interesting happened, he would sneak off to a bathroom and whisper into a tape recorder. Finally, after a year of spying, Cameron finished the book, which he called *Fast Times at Ridgemont High*.

When Universal Studios released a movie based on the book in 1982, it made some waves. *Fast Times at Ridgemont High* showed what life was *really* like for teens—Cameron didn't hide the wild and crazy, and often painful, times he experienced at the high school—but many parents didn't want to see it...or believe it. Even with the controversy, the movie was a hit. It's still considered a cult classic and has been watched by thousands of kids and adults around the world.

Cameron went on to write and direct many more successful films, including *Say Anything, Singles, Jerry Maguire,* and *Almost Famous,* the story of his own life as a teenage rock reporter. Cameron, now more than "almost famous" himself, still writes and directs from his heart. His life was full of bold leaps, into journalism, then novels, then movies. And with each leap, Cameron showed the world that faith in yourself and a positive outlook can make anything possible.

How Will You Rock the World?

I am going to rock the world by becoming an actor. I think I am really good at acting and that it will be a good career. My hero is Jackie Chan because he is so cool and funny. He started off with just little movies that nobody has heard of and now he has movies like Rumble in the Bronx and Mr. Nice Guy. I want to become an actor because I grew up on movies.

Michael McGonegal, age 12

Sammy Sosa

1968 – ✢ Baseball Player ✢
The Dominican Republic

My biggest mistake was trading Sammy Sosa.

—PRESIDENT GEORGE W. BUSH,
WHO FORMERLY OWNED SAMMY'S FIRST BASEBALL TEAM,
THE TEXAS RANGERS.

Sammy burst into the kitchen, grinning from ear to ear. His mother was at the stove, fanning herself to keep cool in the muggy heat. He glanced around at his six brothers and sisters crammed into a single room and thought, *I hate this place.* The tin roof, the dirt floor, the smell of garbage. . .for years he had dreamed of buying his family a nice, big, clean house to live in. And three huge meals a day to fill their bellies.

"Mama," he said quietly, holding a piece of paper out to her, "we're millionaires." She took the check from his hand and stared at it for the longest time, as tears began streaming down her face. For the Sosa family, it might as well have been a million dollars. The check was for over three thousand dollars—more than Sammy's mother could earn in years of working as a maid. *Maybe God has finally heard my prayers*, she thought.

Maybe indeed. Her son, Sammy Sosa, had just signed his first pro baseball contract. . .and he was just sixteen years old!

Back home, Sammy is called Mikey. His grandmother heard the name on a soap opera and gave it to him as a nickname. ❖

This future baseball legend was born in the Dominican Republic, an island nation in the Caribbean. Sammy's father drove a tractor in the sugarcane fields that cover the island, and his mother cleaned the houses of the wealthy. Sammy was just six when his father died suddenly from cancer, changing his world overnight.

With eight mouths to feed, everyone in the family had to work. Sammy left home in the dark early mornings to shine shoes, went to school during the day, spent evenings washing cars, and returned home long after the sun set. He gave every penny he earned to his mother, but many nights the family still went to bed hungry. These hard times changed Sammy forever:

> When you don't have any control over your economic situation, when your stomach is empty, when you see your mother working so hard. . .it leaves a mark on you.

He vowed he would pull himself and his family out of poverty one day.

When the family moved from their small village to a larger city, things got even worse. The eight of them crowded into a one-bedroom shack with dirt floors and no indoor plumbing. The streets were covered in trash and raw sewage. Sammy worked hard shining shoes. One customer, American businessman Bill Chase, was so impressed with Sammy and his brothers' hard work that he hired them to sweep the floors of his factory. Sammy got paid about $20 a week—a huge improvement on his shoe-shining money. At thirteen, he knew his mother had no money for college, and he didn't have time to take this job *and* go to classes, so he quit school.

Although he was sad to quit school, the decision had one good outcome: more time to play baseball! Baseball is the national sport of the

Dominican Republic. "In my country small boys begin playing baseball not long after they learn to walk." Sammy hadn't played much as a kid, he was too busy working, but when Bill heard he was learning to play, he bought Sammy his first baseball glove.

Now he had a focus: He knew that some Dominicans got into the major leagues and that there was money to be made. . .but only if he was great. He talked Bill into giving his other brothers extra hours sweeping so that he could devote more time to practice. "For me there weren't any days off." remembered Sammy, "I worked at baseball every day." He played in the streets and dirt lots, using sticks for bats and balled-up rags, stuffed corn husks and even old milk cartons for baseballs.

Although he started playing baseball later than most Dominican kids, Sammy worked harder than anyone else. After just a year of playing, the fourteen-year-old was attracting crowds, and even television cameras, to his games. When jealous players said he was crazy to dream of playing in the major leagues, Sammy ignored them and worked even harder.

> Most baseball players have superstitious things they do to give them good luck. Sammy "blesses" the field with three drops of coffee before each game. ❖

He auditioned for tons of major league scouts, but got rejected again and again. "You're not fast enough," "You're not strong enough," "You're not big enough," they said. But Sammy didn't give up. The next year, when he turned sixteen, scouts for the Texas Rangers watched him play and invited Sammy to join the team. That's when they gave him the $3500 check—a signing bonus (almost three times his yearly salary), which he gave to his mother, of course. It was his dream come true.

Sammy's whole family went to the airport that day in 1986 when he left for the United States. He was both excited and terrified, and not just because it was his first time in an airplane. Sammy knew he still faced an uphill battle once he reached the U.S. Ninety to ninety-five percent of foreign-born baseball players get sent home after starting in the major leagues. Would he be one of the unlucky majority? Sammy spent years working his way up through the minor leagues, struggling to learn the game and build his strength (eating a more nutritious diet, he bulked up from a skinny 160 pounds to a hulking 210 pounds). All the while he sent every penny of his small salary back home to his family.

But Sammy never got sent home. In 1989, after proving himself in the minor leagues, he was finally invited to play in the major league games. He surprised the whole league with his talent early in the season when he hit a home run against Roger Clemens, one of the best pitchers of all time. It was his first major league home run, but it certainly wouldn't be his last. Sammy was a spotty player at first and was traded several times, first to the Chicago White Sox and then to the Chicago Cubs. But over the years his playing steadily improved. In 1993 he became the first Cub in history to hit thirty-three home runs and steal thirty bases in a single season. Only a few of the greatest players of all time had done that!

> When Sammy first got to the U.S. he couldn't speak or read English. Once, as he was getting ready to eat a can of tuna fish for dinner, an American player stopped him. It wasn't tuna after all—it was cat food! ❖

With the Cubs, Sammy's fame grew, but it wasn't until 1998 that his name became a household word. He and Mark McGuire of the St. Louis Cardinals were neck-and-neck to break Roger Maris' record of 61 home runs in a single season, set in 1961. McGuire was the first to break it in a game against the Cubs, and Sammy proved his generous nature by running in from right field to hug and congratulate McGuire. But just when everyone thought the race was over, Sammy broke Maris' record as well. He was happy to share the glory with McGuire, saying, "He's *the man* in the United States and I am *the man* in the Dominican Republic." In the end, Sammy hit sixty-six home runs to McGuire's seventy, and was voted Most Valuable Player in both the National League and on the All-Star team. He even made the cover of *Sports Illustrated* as Sportsman of the Year.

Sammy was not only a baseball hero, but one of its highest-paid players as well, earning over $10 million a year. He was able to buy his family a new house, and his mother never had to work again. The Dominican Republic named him "Ambassador of Baseball," and even President Bill Clinton honored him in the 1998 State of the Union Address and invited him to the White House to light the national Christmas tree.

Just as he assisted his family, Sammy wanted to help the country he loves. He boosted tourism in the Dominican Republic by starring in commercials encouraging people to travel there. He established a foundation to support needy Dominican families and a medical center to give free medical care to their children. Each year Dominican schools receive more than $500,000 from Sammy, and forty computers for every home run he hits! When a devastating hurricane wiped out many Caribbean communities, Sammy created a fund to get victims back on their feet.

> *I want to be known as a good person more than a good baseball player. I am prouder of my rebuilding efforts than all of my home runs. I love my country. I will do anything I can to help them.*

He also helps out in the United States. His "Sammy Claus World Tour" gives away toys to over 7,000 children. And baseball Sundays at Wrigley Field are now called "Sammy Days" because he donates tickets to low-income kids. In 1998, Sammy was honored for his generosity with the Gene Autry Courage Award for athletes who "demonstrate heroism in the face of adversity and overcome hardships to inspire others."

Sammy's story inspires people in America and around the world. They see that America has embraced this outsider—a black, Spanish-speaking man from the Dominican Republic—as one of its heroes. Sammy has led a movement in baseball towards accepting Latino players, who now make up more than 25% of U.S. teams. But with all his money and fame, Sammy never forgets where he came from. While most major league players practice in state-of-the-art gyms and pristine baseball diamonds, Sammy still practices in his old dirt ball field in the Dominican Republic. Surrounded by the sights, sounds and people he grew up with he can remember the struggles of his childhood, the lessons he has learned, and can see how far he's come.

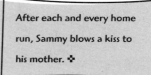

After each and every home run, Sammy blows a kiss to his mother. ❖

Tony Hawk

1 9 6 8 – ✤ S k a t e b o a r d e r ✤ U n i t e d S t a t e s

Skateboarding is not a crime—it's my career.

–TONY HAWK

Eleven-year-old Tony "ollied" (bounced his skateboard) off the top of the ramp, then turned himself around 360°. For a moment he was weightless. The board floated somewhere beneath him as he twisted in the air. Suddenly, Tony planted his feet back on the board and slammed it into the cement surface with a loud, satisfying "thrrack." Just like that, he was at the other end of the ramp flipping himself in the air again like some strange, skinny dolphin.

Nearby, two boys laughed at some inside joke as they slowly rolled around on their skateboards. They were only Duane Peters and Steve Alba, two of the best pro skaters around! They sported an extreme "punk" look, and Tony wanted them to like him more than anything in the world. He skated over and started laughing with them, hoping they might just think he was in on their joke. But they weren't laughing anymore. Instead, they raised their eyebrows, as if to say, "Who's the twerp?" Duane spit, just missing Tony's shoes, "This is punk rock kid."

Steve doubled over laughing. Then Duane started laughing too. Tony was obviously not *in* on the joke. He *was* the joke. He picked up his board and walked slowly out of the park.

Tony knew then that he still had a lot to learn about skating if he was going to be better than those guys. He vowed he would be the best skater in the world, just so he wouldn't have to take that kind of attitude from anyone. And that's just what he did.

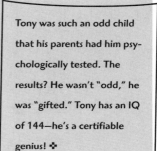

Tony was such an odd child that his parents had him psychologically tested. The results? He wasn't "odd," he was "gifted." Tony has an IQ of 144—he's a certifiable genius! ❖

But before he became the skateboarding champion of the world, Tony describes himself as a complete and total nightmare. "Instead of the terrible twos, I was the terrible youth," he said. "I was a hyper, rail-thin geek on a sugar buzz. My mom summed it up best when she said I was, 'challenging.'" Even as a toddler, he chucked toys at his elderly baby sitter.

Tony was also unusually determined about achieving his goals. His first time at bat in a Little League game, he hit a single. He was stoked! But his next time up, he struck out. Tony immediately took off running across the outfield and disappeared into a ravine at the far end of the field. He stayed there until the game was over and his father bribed him out with an ice-cream sundae. Tony could be a little hard on himself.

In the late sixties and early seventies, skateboarding was actually called "sidewalk surfing." Tony was just six when he first stepped onto an old blue fiberglass "banana board" at the prodding of his brother Steve.

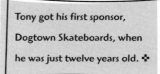

Tony got his first sponsor, Dogtown Skateboards, when he was just twelve years old. ❖

He couldn't figure out how to turn, and whined until his brother taught him how. He was no good at all, but as he says, "something had begun to itch." Tony's extreme energy and determination finally had an outlet.

By the fourth grade, the itch had gotten so bad that Tony formed a skating group with his neighborhood buddies and visited his first skatepark, fittingly named Oasis. He begged for a membership, but instead, his dad built him a ramp of his own in their driveway.

The next year, Tony's mom finally let him skate at Oasis after much convincing. The park swarmed with guys doing tricks, always looking like they were about to run into each another. Tony had to rent his safety equipment, which had often been worn by four guys in a single day. The elbow and kneepads were always soggy and stinky with other people's sweat. Padded up like a gladiator, he walked into the skating area. The tricks these guys were doing seemed impossible. How would he ever be able to do that stuff?

> Tony was so skinny when he first started skating that regular knee pads slid right off him. He had to use elbow pads instead, and even those slipped during his runs! ❖

Well, it only took Tony a couple years to master all their tricks, plus invent a whole bunch of his own: the fakie to frontside rock and the frontside 540/rodeo flip (during which a skater does almost two whole rotations in the air). The reason Tony was so good? He was obsessed. He ate, lived and breathed skateboarding, even though most people considered the sport "uncool" in the early eighties.

A group of professional skaters practiced at Oasis. Tony became friends with them and then joined their team, "The Bones Brigade," just before his thirteenth birthday. Most skaters in the group were seventeen or eighteen years old, and twelve-year-old Tony was a bit intimidated to be skating with his idols. But the team manager, ex-world champion Stacy Peralta, had secretly been watching him for a year and recognized his "fierce determination." He had no worries about putting the kid on the team.

> Tony has invented over eighty tricks! ❖

Tony started out skating as an amateur for the Bones Brigade, and his first competitions were disappointing. As he puts it, "I sucked for a while." He was barely over four feet tall and weighed just eighty pounds: "the walking noodle," as he called himself. But even though he wasn't the best skater on the team, Tony had his moments of glory. Like when he picked up his favorite magazine, *Thrasher,* and saw a picture of himself doing a lien-to-tail on the cover. He had no idea anyone had even snapped the photo!

In 1982, at fourteen, Tony's dream finally came true; he became a professional skateboarder. But he still had a long way to go. He had a hard time getting air because he was so skinny and couldn't build the momentum he needed at the end of a half-pipe. But Tony was creative: to get more height, he would ollie into the air, bouncing his board off the end of the pipe. It worked, but some skaters

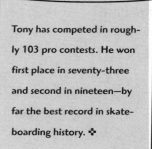

Tony has competed in roughly 103 pro contests. He won first place in seventy-three and second in nineteen—by far the best record in skateboarding history. ❖

got on his case for skating like "a geek." It would take a few wins before anyone took Tony Hawk, the "geeky" fourteen-year-old pro, seriously.

While Tony was struggling up the ranks of the skateboarding world in the afternoons and on weekends, he was also struggling through the ranks of high school. Skateboarding was still uncool, and no one at school really knew (or cared) that Tony was a professional skateboarder. Tony was an easy target for the jocks to ridicule: he was scrawny and dressed in weird skater clothes. Back then the skateboarding style meant lots of skulls, baggy shorts and duct-taped shoes. Everybody else was wearing skin-tight designer jeans!

Skating became Tony's only sanctuary. Over the next few years, Tony skated in more and more competitions... he even began to win. In Tony's first professional win, he actually beat Duane Peters, the very same skater who spit at him years before. It was a sweet victory for Tony, the first of many.

By the age of sixteen, Tony was winning all the time. He was the undisputed skateboarding champion of the world and his life got a whole lot better. He was no longer scrawny; at six feet, four inches tall, Tony towered over most kids at school. They finally left him alone. Skateboarding was also starting to get popular, so Tony was earning quite a bit of money from all his sponsorships. By his senior year in high school Tony bought himself a house! Best of all, Tony felt he was skating up to his own standards—he was achieving his goals, landing tricks and inventing new ones.

Tony dominated the skating world for years. By 1991 he had achieved so many of his goals and won so many contests, that he felt it was time for a break. He retired and formed a skateboard company called Birdhouse. But Tony was never one to go quietly. He still had one more trick up his sleeve before he was through: the "900."

The 900 is probably the most difficult skateboarding trick known to man. It requires three full rotations in the air, and of course, a successful landing. Tony had been trying to do this trick since 1986, and had one cracked rib and a crooked spinal cord to show for it. But in 1999, at the ripe old age of thirty-one (positively *ancient* in the skateboarding world), Tony landed the 900 at the X Games. The crowd roared as his buddies dog-piled on top of him—no skater on earth had ever landed it! It officially put Tony into "skateboarding god" status.

Since then, Tony has created more goals for himself and achieved every one. He's been in movies, ads, and most recently, his own video game: *Tony Hawk Pro Skater*. It is one of the highest-rated video games ever, and the closest most humans will ever get to landing a "frontside twist madonna." And he still skates every day. Thanks to Tony, skateboarding is more popular than ever, and has paved the way for other alternative sports like snowboarding and surfing. Tony is a great role model for anyone who wants to push their limits.

How Will You Rock the World?

I will rock the world by being a bike rider who does tricks. I will also be a snowboarder. I'm already practicing both. I like to snowboard with my friends and last time we went I did a kick flip off the ramp. If I become

famous with my dirt bike racing or with snowboarding I would tell everyone that I appreciate the encouragement my mom and dad have given me and also the help my brother has given me.

Brett Cox, age 10

Tiger Woods

1975– ✤ Golfer ✤ United States

All I can do is keep trying to get better.
Every day is about making little adjustments,
taking what you've got on that day
and finding the way to deal with it.

—TIGER WOODS

The six-year-old planted his feet, and putted the golf ball across the living room carpet into a tipped-over cup. His favorite cassette tape was playing, the one he'd begged his parents to buy for him. It wasn't rap, it wasn't reggae. What he heard as he putted ball after ball was:

MY DECISIONS ARE STRONG!
I DO IT WITH ALL MY HEART!
I FOCUS AND GIVE IT MY ALL!

These words were buried beneath the recorded sounds of rippling water and heavenly flutes. They were messages to his unconscious mind, meant to inspire and motivate him to achieve his goals. In the case of six-year-old Tiger Woods, the goal was to be the best golfer ever.

Tiger's real name is Eldrick, a combination of his parents' names: Earl and Kultida. But from his birth, everyone called him Tiger. His dad gave him that nickname to honor his friend, Nguyen Phong, a South Vietnamese soldier that Earl had fought beside in Vietnam. Earl had called Nguyen "Tiger" because he was so fearless.

By age six, Tiger Woods was already listening to get mentally tough, like the first Tiger, so that he could improve his golf game. He had been winning at golf since the age of three, but he kept his focus on improving, never satisfied by any tournament's success. By twenty-four he had achieved his goal: he was the number-one ranked golfer in the world.

Tiger's dad started playing golf in his forties. He loved the game and got to be pretty good, but he believed that the key to really mastering any sport was to start early. When his son Tiger was born, Earl got to test his theory. As Earl hit balls into a net in the garage, Tiger would watch. The baby was so into it, that his mom, Kultida, had to move his high chair into the garage and feed him out there while Earl hit practice shots. By the time he was one year old, Tiger was ready to play! Earl and Kultida took him to a nearby golf course, where he practiced hitting balls, and then rested afterwards in his stroller, drinking from his bottle.

At two, Tiger was already a phenomenon. He beat comedian and amateur golfer Bob Hope in a putting contest on national television. When his dad would take him to the local course, he'd comment on the form of other players, "Look Daddy, that man has a reverse pivot!" While Earl wanted Tiger to be a golfer, it was only because Tiger wanted it so badly himself. Earl didn't want to burn Tiger out on golf, so he never pushed him to practice. Instead, he waited for Tiger to call *him* at work

Tiger stays incredibly cool and calm under pressure. Maybe that's thanks to his mom. Once, while watching tennis star John McEnroe throw a tantrum during a tennis match, on TV, she told her young son never to act like that. "I [won't] have my reputation as a parent ruined!" she warned. ❖

each day to ask "Daddy, can I practice with you?" Earl believes that for anyone to succeed, the desire to practice must come from within and prides himself on never having to ask Tiger to practice. As Tiger says, "The best thing about those early practices was that my father always kept it fun."

After Tiger shot a 48 on a nine-hole course when he was only three, Earl decided to let Tiger enter his first tournament, and hired a professional coach. From then on, Tiger's childhood was filled with "youngest evers"—at eight he was the youngest-ever champion of the Optimists International Junior World golf tournament; at fifteen, the youngest ever to win the U.S. Junior National Amateur; at eighteen, the youngest-ever winner of the U.S. Amateur Championship; and then, at twenty-one, the age he turned professional (able to accept money for play), he was the youngest winner ever of the prestigious Masters Tournament.

Starting early helped Tiger's game, for sure, but he also lucked out when it came to genes–as an adult, Tiger's 6'2" height and 180 lbs. let him smack the ball with real power. But probably most important to Tiger's success is his mental toughness. And that toughness didn't just happen naturally. Listening to tapes was just one way Tiger focused his mind.

When Tiger was just seven, Earl decided to test his son's concentration by using some of the psychological warfare tricks he'd learned as a soldier in Vietnam. These tricks were designed to confuse the enemy and make him doubt himself. As Tiger prepared to hit the ball, his dad would stand fifteen feet in front of him, and say, "I'm a tree." Tiger would have to hit over him. When Tiger was concentrating on a bunker shot, Earl would loudly jingle the change in his pocket. And when Tiger had a crucial putt to make, Earl would suddenly unfasten the Velcro strap on his

> Tiger was being photographed for a *Sports Illustrated* cover with a 650 pound Bengal tiger, Samson. The tiger was agitated and growling until it saw Tiger, who confidently walked up and began cuddling with the cat. The tiger's trainer said, "That young man projects confidence like I've never seen. You can't fake that with a big cat. Samson sensed no weakness or fear in Tiger, just power and inner peace." ❖

glove with a loud rrrrrip. Earl tried to annoy, harass, and bug his son, all to help Tiger focus his mind. It must have worked. Tiger's concentration is so intense that today he hears nothing when he's on the course, saying, "My only thought is to hit solid golf shots all day long."

This mental attitude allowed Tiger to take the biggest risk of his career—just when everything was going perfectly for him, he decided it was time for a change. He was twenty, had just turned professional, and had been offered endorsement contracts from Nike and Titleist, among others, that totaled over $60 million. He had won four out of his first fifteen professional tournaments and had earned $1.8 million in prize money. He was at the top of his game—and the top of the world. For anyone else, this would've been *it*—a lifetime high, a place to look down from and say, "I did it!" Not Tiger. Something just didn't seem right to him.

His next big tournament was the Masters, in Augusta, Georgia, in 1997. Against the best golfers in the world, he won by a record twelve strokes. What did he think about that? Well, as he told his friends afterwards, "My swing really sucks."

> Tiger is 1/4 Chinese, 1/4 African American, 1/4 Thai, 1/8 American Indian, and 1/8 Caucasian. Because more and more Americans share Tiger's situation, there has been talk in Congress of drafting a "Tiger Woods Bill" to create a new category of race (like black, white, Asian) called "multi-ethnic." ❖

He decided it was time to revamp his swing. This was a risky thing to do: in the history of golf, some champions who had changed their swing never returned to their former glory. Also, he knew he'd get worse before he'd get better, and there was the real chance of public humiliation. A lot of people were waiting for him to fail, thinking, "Okay this young black kid won some tournaments as an amateur, but now he's in the big time." They were waiting for him to choke.

Tiger knew this, but he also knew who he was—fearless, just like the first Tiger. He ignored everyone who said he was crazy to mess with success. He worked with his coach, swung his club a few hundred thousand times, and watched countless videos of his swing. In the next nineteen months after the 1997 Masters, Tiger won just one event. Despite the critics' murmurings about "flash in the pan," Tiger stayed calm. As he put it, "Winning is not always the barometer of getting better."

In May 1999, after more than a year and a half of work, Tiger finally felt he had it—the swing that he wanted. He roared back, winning ten out of the next fourteen events he competed in, and was ranked number one in the world.

Tiger Woods has done more than just win games, however. He has electrified the stuffy world of golf, and forced it to change. With his strength and athleticism challenging the old ways, paunchy bellies (and bad pants!) are disappearing from the game. Instead, the winners are now players, like Tiger, who are stronger and more disciplined.

These changes in the world of golf also fit with the goal of the Tiger Woods Foundation, which he started in 1996: to bring more kids, especially minority kids, into a game that used to be for rich whites. Tiger's foundation strives to make golf courses and equipment more accessible to poor kids.

> Tiger's career tournament earnings as of 3/15/01: $22,461,206. ❖

He hopes with his example and through the clinics he teaches, that golf "will attract the better natural athlete." As Tiger said, "Just imagine if Michael Jordan, with his size and strength and hand-eye coordination, had started playing golf early." Like his dad, Tiger believes kids need to be exposed early to sports. He thinks sports are a way for kids to learn a lot of lessons about life. As he says, "Golf has been good to me, and the lessons I've learned...I'm trying to pass on and show kids how to apply them to every aspect of life. Do your best. Play fairly. Embrace every activity with integrity, honesty and discipline. Be responsible for your actions. And above all, have fun."

Iqbal Masih / Craig Kielburger

1983-1995 ✤ Pakistan /
1983- ✤ Canada
Child Labor Activists

For about $12, Iqbal Masih was sold into slavery as a carpet weaver when he was just four years old. Six years later he made a daring escape from his work prison and began to speak out against child slavery. He asked the world to help him achieve freedom and an education for all Pakistani children. Iqbal caught the attention of many child rights activists and won the Reebok Human Rights Youth in Action Award in 1994.

By showing the world the horrible truth of forced child labor, Iqbal made many friends around the world. But he also made enemies. In 1995, the brave child labor activist was murdered at the age of twelve.

On the other side of the globe, Iqbal's death so profoundly affected a Canadian boy that he too became a spokesperson against child labor. Twelve-year-old Craig Kielburger gathered together a group of friends and founded the organization (Kids Can) Free the Children, now the world's largest network of children helping children, with over 100,000 kid members in 27 countries around the world.

For the past five years, Craig has traveled to more than 30 countries, visiting street children and factories, and addressing government officials and business leaders, educators and students around the world. Free the Children has initiated projects all over the world, like the construction of more than 100 schools and many live-in rehabilitation centers for children. Most importantly, Craig's organization has started leadership programs for youth, and projects to help unite youth from all over the world to join in the fight. Craig and Iqbal show the power of kids banding together to change the world!

David Leung
1982- ✤ Investor ✤ United States

David brought home his fifth grade report card: good grades again. Instead of rewarding him with a new CD or computer game, his parents decided to try something new. They gave David one hundred shares of stock, thinking it would be a good way for him to get involved in saving up for college. There was just one hitch: David had to do some research to figure out which company's stock to buy, and then he'd have to convince his parents that he'd made a good choice.

David went to the library and used Value Line, a free investment guide, to research possible companies. He found one that looked pretty good: Microsoft. Good choice—that's the company that made Bill Gates the richest person in the world! Every year after that, his parents gave him one hundred more shares to invest. He also bought stocks with just about every dollar he made doing after-school jobs. Eight years later, David's stocks were worth close to $500,000.

How did he do it? David says it wasn't so hard. He shares his investing know-how with anyone who wants to know at his two websites: Investing for Kids (*http.///library.thinkquest.org/3096*) and Invest Smart (*http://library.thinkquest.org/10326*), a site that includes a stock investment game used in more than 9,000 schools in the United States.

What's David secret? Easy: spend less so you'll have more money to invest. As David says, "It doesn't matter how much you save, as long as you get in the habit." He puts almost every dollar he earns into stocks. And he suggests when your parents ask you what you want, ask for "Nike stock, instead of Nike shoes." If you take David's advice, you'll be able to buy not just one pair of Nikes, but a whole truckload.

Jonny Lang

1981- ❖ Blues Musician ❖
United States

Jon Langseth, Jr. grew up in Fargo, North Dakota, about as far from the blues as a boy can get. He always loved music and even played the saxophone in his junior high band. But he knew almost nothing about the blues, a soulful music created nearly a hundred years ago by black musicians in the South—their response to the misery of slavery.

At age twelve, Jon saw his first blues band, Bad Medicine, and fell in love with the sound. After begging his parents for a guitar, Jon began taking lessons from Bad Medicine's guitarist. He was so good that within a few months not only did Bad Medicine invite him to join the band, but they renamed themselves Kid Jonny Lang and the Big Bang. It wasn't long before the major labels heard about the teenage blues prodigy.

At age fifteen, Jonny signed a contract with A&M Records, and just before his sixteenth birthday he released his first album, *Lie to Me*. It was a hit and sold over a million copies. Jonny shot to #1 on Billboard's New Artist chart, won Best New Guitarist in *Guitar* magazine and was flooded with invitations to play with music legends like Aerosmith, the Rolling Stones, and B.B. King. It was his dream come true.

Another of Jonny's dreams is to help make the blues popular with kids his own age. On his second album, *Wander This World*, he broke with blues tradition and added new soul and funk sounds to his songs. As musician Luther Allison explains, "Jonny Lang has the power to move the music into the next millennium by reaching the ears of a new generation."

Ben Smilowitz

1981- ✤ Activist ✤ United States

Fifteen-year-old Ben Smilowitz was excited about the Rotary's youth conference, a day-long forum that provided students from around Connecticut and Massachusetts an opportunity to meet and discuss student issues. Inspired by the conference's success, Ben and his friends decided to create the first national, pro-youth organization made up entirely of kids. Ben's organization, the International Student Activism Alliance (ISAA), attracted tons of teens from across the country to work together on protecting student's rights.

As president of the ISAA, Ben used the Internet to connect with student activists all over America and to set up ISAA chapters in every state. One of ISAA's major projects was to get two student representatives onto the Connecticut State Board of Education. At first, the board was skeptical of including student representatives, but because of Ben's work, the Connecticut legislature eventually passed a law allowing two students to hold positions on the board.

Ben and the ISAA have continued to fight for young people's right to express their views and opinions. Kids can't vote, but they should have a say about the world they live in. By the time Ben graduated from high school, the ISAA had grown to over 2,000 members! In 1999, Ben was invited to the White House by President Clinton and appeared on national TV to debate student issues. Now a junior in college, Ben has started a new student's rights organization for high school and college kids and continues to fight for the civil rights of America's youth. As Ben explains, "If you don't step up and make your voice heard, someone else is going to do it for you."

Paul Gordon

1981 – ✤ Director ✤ United States

Paul Gordon is a guy with many passions. At the age of eight, he started making his own movies. At fifteen, he raised $24,000 for a young boy, Eric Graeves, to have a liver transplant. He even stayed overnight at the hospital while Eric had the surgery. The next year Paul raised an additional $59,000 for children in need of transplants and lobbied the U.S. Congress to increase awareness about organ donations.

And that was just high school. At seventeen, Paul wrote, directed, and edited a film about youth violence called *Silhouettes of Time*, which will air on HBO in 2001. The movie was his response to the shootings at Columbine High School. "The only thing you [should] shoot with is a camera," says the young filmmaker. Paul's film encourages teens to make positive choices and to help each other in times of need.

Paul knows that kids have the power to change the world (he's doing it himself, after all). His newest film project is a miniseries about kids doing inspirational things in their communities and he has even written a book called *There Is Hope Left For America's Youth*. Paul spends much of his free time speaking at high schools and middle schools across America on youth violence issues. He hopes to continue making films that are not only entertaining but that have a positive message.

But Paul's passions don't even stop there. He dreams of one day becoming President of the United States. He has already proved that he can accomplish whatever he puts his mind to, so keep your ears open for his name during some future Presidential election.

How Will You Rock the World?

Write your dreams here:

Put your photo here:

Name:

Age:

Address:

Phone number (so we can call you if you win):

Cut out or photocopy this page and send it to:
Boys Who Rocked the World
Beyond Words Publishing, Inc.
20827 N.W. Cornell Road, Suite 500
Hillsboro, Oregon 97124-9808

You could be included in the next book!

Bibliography

Adair, Gene. *Thomas Alva Edison: Inventing the Electric Age.* New York: Oxford University Press, 1996.

Aldred, Cyril. *Tutankhamun's Egypt.* New York: Charles Scribner's Sons, 1972.

Baldwin, Neil. *Edison: Inventing the Century.* New York: Hyperion, 1995.

Beahm, George. *America's Best Loved Boogeyman: Stephen King.* Kansas City: Andrews McMeel Publishing, 1999.

Beahm, George. *Stephen King Country.* Philadelphia: Running Press, 1999.

"Ben Smilowitz" http://www.ussu.org/ben/home.htm (19 January 2001).

Berry, James. *The Berlin Olympics: 1936 Black American Athletes Counter Nazi Propaganda.* New York: Franklin Watts, 1975.

Boardingham, Robert. *The Young Picasso.* New York: Universe Publishing, 1997.

"Braille, The Magic Wand of the Blind," Helen Keller, *New York Times Magazine,* November 11, 1929; from the American Foundation for the Blind website http://afb.org

Brier, Bob. *The Murder of Tutankhamen.* New York: G.P. Putman's Sons, 1998.

Burch, Joann J. *Chico Mendes: Defender of the Rain Forest.* Brookfield, CT: Millbrook Press, 1994.

"Changing His Stripes," *Time* Magazine, vol. 156, no. 7, August 14, 2000, pp. 52-61.

Cobb, Vicki. *Truth on Trial: The Story of Galileo Galilei.* New York: Coward, McCann & Geoghegan, 1979.

"eBraille: Making Braille Easy Around the World," paper given at 66th IFLA Council and General Conference, August 13,2000; www.duxburysystems.com/news.asp

"Explaining Groening: One-on-one with the Sultan of Fun." http://www.labyrinth.net.au/~kwyjibo/matt.html (8 January 2001).

Feinstein, Barry, Daniel Kramer and Jim Marshall. *Early Dylan.* Boston: Bullfinch Press, 1999.

Ford, Barbara. *Howard Carter: Searching for King Tut.* New York: W.H. Freeman and Company, 1995.

Freedman, Russell. *The Life and Death of Crazy Horse.* New York: Holiday House, 1996.

Freedman, Russell. *Out of Darkness: The Story of Louis Braille*. New York: Clarion Books, 1997.

"The Game of Risk: How the Best Golfer in the World Got Even Better," *Time* Magazine, vol. 156, no. 7, August 14, 2000, pp. 57-61.

Garrity, John. *Tiger Woods: The Making of a Champion*. New York: Simon & Schuster, 1996.

Green, Robert. *Tutankhamun*. New York: Franklin Watts, 1996.

Guttmacher, Peter. *Crazy Horse*. New York: Chelsea House Publishers, 1994.

Hardorff, Richard G. *The Surrender and Death of Crazy Horse: A Source Book About the Tragic Episode in Lakota History*. Spokane, WA: The Arthur H. Clark Company, 1998.

"Hawk: Occupation: Skateboarder" http://www.teenreads.com/reviews/0060198605.asp (26 February 2001).

Hoving, Thomas. *The Untold Story of Tutankhamun*. New York: Simon and Schuster, 1978.

Hughes, Libby. *Nelson Mandela: Voice of Freedom*, NY: Dillon Press, 1992.

Humphries, Patrick. *Absolutely Dylan*. New York: Viking Studio, 1991.

Ireland, Karin. *Albert Einstein*. Englewood Cliffs, NJ: Silver Burdett Press, 1989.

Josephson, Judith Pinkerton. *Jesse Owens: Track and Field Legend*. Springfield, NJ: Enslow Publishers, 1997.

Kerst, Friedrich. *Mozart: The Man and the Artist Revealed in His Own Words*. New York: Dover Publications, 1965.

King, Stephen. *On Writing*. New York: Scribner, 2000.

Koenig, Viviane. *The Ancient Egyptians: Life in the Nile Valley*. Brookfield, CT: The Millbrook Press, 1992.

Komroff, Manuel. *Mozart*. New York: Alfred A. Knopf, 1956.

Lee, Bruce. *Striking Thoughts: Bruce Lee's Wisdom for Everyday Living*. Boston: Turtle Publishing, 2000.

Lee, Bruce. *Words From a Master*. Chicago: Contemporary Books, 1999.

Lesinski, Jeanne. *Bill Gates.* Minneapolis: Lerner Publications Company, 2000.

"The Long Walk of Nelson Mandela"
http://www.pbs.org/wgbh/pages/frontline/shows/mandela/ (12 February 2001).

MacLachlan, James. *Galileo Galilei.* New York: Oxford University Press, 1997.

Mailer, Norman. *Portrait of Picasso as a Young Man.* New York: Atlantic Monthly Press, 1995.

Mandela, Nelson. *Mandela: An Illustrated Autobiography.* Boston: Little, Brown & Co., 1994.

"Matt Groening Biography" Mr. Showbiz Celebrities http://mr.showbiz.go.com/people/mattgroening/content/bio.html (8 January 2001).

McPherson, Stephanie. *Ordinary Genius: The Story of Albert Einstein.* Minneapolis: Carolrhoda Books, Inc., 1995.

McNeill, Sarah. *Ancient Egyptian People.* Brookfield, CT: The Millbrook Press, 1996.

"Microsoft's Fiscal Millennium" http://www.fool.com/news/2000/msft000728.htm (28 July 2000).

Millard, Anne. *The World of the Pharaoh.* New York: Peter Bedrick Books, 1998.

Mitchell, Barbara. *The Wizard of Sound: A Story about Thomas Edison.* Minneapolis, Carolrhoda Books, 1997.

"The Mother Jones Interview: Matt Groening" MoJo Wire
http://www.motherjones.com/mother_jones/MA99/groening.html (8 January 2001).

Muhlberger, Richard. *What Makes a Picasso a Picasso?* New York: Viking, 1994.

Murdoch. David. *Tutankhamun: The Life and Death of the Pharaoh.* New York: DK Publishing, 1998.

Nuwer, Hank. *The Legend of Jesse Owens.* New York: Franklin Watts, 1998.

Owens, Jesse. *Blackthink: My Life As Black Man and White Man.* New York: William Morrow, 1970.

Parker, Steve. *Thomas Edison and Electricity.* NewYork: Harper Collins, 1992.

Rees, Rosemary. *The Ancient Egyptians.* Crystal Lake, IL: Heinemann Library, 1997.

Reino, Joseph. *Stephen King: The First Decade, Carrie to Pet Sematary.* Boston: Twayne Publishers, 1988.

Revkin, Andrew. *The Burning Season: The Murder of Chico Mendes and the Fight for the Amazon Rain Forest.* Boston: Houghton Mifflin, 1990.

Richmond, Ray and Antonia Coffman, eds. *The Simpsons: A Complete Guide to our Favorite Family*. New York: HarperCollins, 1997.

Roberts, Russell. *The Rulers of Ancient Egypt*. San Diego, CA: Lucent Books, 1999.

Saidman, Anne. *Stephen King: Master of Horror*. Minneapolis: Lerner Publications Company, 1992.

Severance, John B. *Einstein: Visionary Scientist*. New York: Clarion Books, 1999.

Shoumatoff, Alex. *The World is Burning: Murder in the Rain Forest*. Boston: Little, Brown and Company, 1990.

Spitz, Bob. *Dylan: A Biography*. New York: McGraw-Hill, 1989.

St. George, Judith. *Crazy Horse*. New York: G.P. Putman's Sons, 1994.

Sullivan, George. *Great Lives: Sports*. New York: Charles Scribner's Sons, 1988.

Teague, Allison L. *Prince of the Fairway: The Tiger Woods Story*, Greensboro, NC: Avisson Press, Inc., 1997.

"The Tiger Woods Official Golf Website" http://ww1.sportsline.com (5 January 2001).

"*Time 100,*" *Time* magazine, April 13, 1998.

"Wall Street Kid," *Los Angeles Times* article dated January 24, 2000, from *http:library.thinkquest.org/3096/david.htm*

Wallace, James and Jim Erickson. *Hard Drive: Bill Gates and the Making of the Microsoft Empire*. New York: John Wiley & Sons, Inc., 1992.

"William H. Gates: Before Microsoft" http://ei.cs.vt.edu/~history/Gates.Mirick.html (8 August 2000)

"'What is Braille?' American Foundation for the Blind" http://afb.org/info (15 December 2000).

White, Michael and John Gibbin. *Einstein: A Life in Science*. New York: Dutton Publishing, 1993.

White, Michael. *Galileo Galilei: Inventor, Astronomer and Rebel*. Woodbridge, CT: Blackbirch Press, 1999.

Woods, Earl and Pete McDaniel, *Training a Tiger: A Father's Guide to Raising a Winner in Both Golf and Life*. New York: HarperCollins, 1997.

Wukovits, John F. *Stephen King*. San Diego, CA: Lucas Books, 1999.

Young, Penny. *Mozart*. New York: The Bookwright Press, 1988.

Other Books by Beyond Words Publishing

EVER IMAGINE CREATING YOUR OWN COMIC BOOKS?
Why just imagine? Make it happen!
Get great tips on:

- Starting a studio and choosing the right tools

- Creating your own characters and stories

- Developing your drawing techniques

Create your own comic books and let your imagination soar!

144 pages, black and white art, $9.95 softcover

IS THERE A ROCK STAR IN THE HOUSE?
It could be you! All you budding musicologists, get the scoop on:

- Choosing the perfect name for your band

- Finding song ideas

- Creating a demo tape

✳ Scholastic & Book of the Month Club Selection ✳

How did Britney Spears get her start? This book won't tell you that, but it will inspire you to live your rock and roll dream: from how to start a band, to how to get discovered, and everything in between (like finding the perfect look and attitude to express your musical soul, and, of course, getting your parents on board to the whole idea of you as a rock star). Written by a former teenage rocker, with advice from twenty real kid bands. Rock on!

152 pages, black and white art, $8.95 softcover

DO YOU HAVE THE "WRITE" STUFF?

Ever dreamed of becoming a famous author? In *So, You Wanna Be a Writer?* learn the ins and outs of getting your work published from famous writers like Michael Crichton, Amelia Atwater-Rhodes, and Wendelin Van Draanen. Plus, meet ten real kid authors who share their best writing tips and advice!

Writer wannabes will learn:
- how to begin a career in writing
- exploring different areas of writing: poetry, journalism, fiction, or nonfiction
- where to find inspiration for your stories
- a current and thorough list of magazines, web-sites, contests, and book publishers looking for kid authors

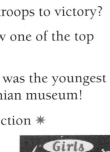

160 pages, black and white art, $8.95 softcover

GREAT STORIES OF REAL GIRLS WHO MADE HISTORY!

Did you know that:
- Joan of Arc was only 17 when she led the French troops to victory?

- Cristen Powell started drag racing at 16 and is now one of the top drag racers in America?

- Wang Yani began painting at the age of three? She was the youngest artist ever to have her own exhibit at the Smithsonian museum!

✳ Scholastic & Book of the Month Club Selection ✳

Girls Who Rocked the World lets you get to know these incredible teen-age girls and many more. This is the first book ever to set girls' history straight by telling the stories of inspiring young heroines.

And impress your girlfriends with even more great stories of women heroines with *Girls Who Rocked the World 2*.

✳ A Troll Book Club Selection ✳

So. . .how are you going to rock the world?

160 pages, black and white illustrations, $8.95 softcover

DO YOU KNOW THE REAL YOU?

Everywhere you turn, teen magazines are telling you how to look and who you're supposed to be. Shouldn't YOU be the authority on yourself? Sixteen-year-old Sarah Stillman offers an escape from superficiality in her book *Soul Searching: A Girl's Guide to Finding Herself.*
Learn how to:

- Create a calming atmosphere for yourself through Feng Shui and Aromatherapy
- Relax with yoga and meditation

- Keep a journal and analyze your dreams

- Find your passions and accomplish your goals

It's time to start discovering yourself—you never know what you might find!

140 pages, black and white art, $10.95 softcover

DOES YOUR MEOWER HAVE PSYCHIC POWER?
DOES FIDO KNOW THINGS YOU DON'T KNOW?

Do you dare to explore the uncharted world of your pet's brain? Read about:

- Spooky stories of pets with psychic powers

- Tests to find out if your pet is psychic

- Ways to increase your pet's psychic abilities

- Astrology charts for your pet

✳ Scholastic & Book of the Month Club Selection ✳

Can your cat get out of the house even when all the doors are closed? Has your dog ever seen a ghost? Does your horse seem to read your mind? If you can answer yes to any of these questions, you might have (are you sitting down?) a psychic pet! Better keep that food dish filled from now on!

124 pages, black and white art, $7.95 softcover

KIDSMAKINGMONEY.COM

Okay, *Better Than a Lemonade Stand* by fifteen-year-old author Daryl Bernstein is not a guide to high tech riches. But computers aren't the only way to get rich quick. Daryl started his first business when he was only eight! Since then, he has tried all fifty-one of the kid businesses in this book, all of which are easy to start up. Today, Daryl runs his own multimillion-dollar business and is happy to share with you the secrets of his success. Learn how you can earn bucks by being a:

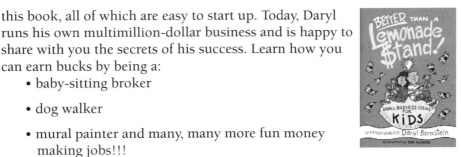

- baby-sitting broker

- dog walker

- mural painter and many, many more fun money making jobs!!!

※ A Doubleday Book Club Selection ※

150 pages, black and white cartoon illustrations, $9.95 softcover

EXCUSES! EXCUSES!

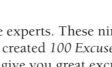

Authors Mike and Zach are excuse experts. These nine- and ten-year-old best friends have created *100 Excuses for Kids*, a hysterical book which will give you great excuses for getting out of anything—vegetables, homework, chores whatever! Get the latest and newest excuses for:

- Going to bed late

- Not eating your vegetables

- Not cleaning your room and many (97 to be exact), many more!

※ Scholastic Book Club Selection ※

96 pages, black and white cartoon art, $5.95 softcover

HEY, GUYS! EVERYTHING YOU NEED TO KNOW, ACCORDING TO THE "EXPERTS"— GUYS JUST LIKE YOU!

Read about:

- tips on catching frogs, bugs, and other creatures

- wise-cracks to make your buddies laugh

- the scoop on girls

From making comic strips to dealing with girls, *Boys Know It All* is packed with great ideas from thirty-two cool guys —just like you!

160 pages, black and white collage art, $8.95 softcover

HEY, GIRLS!
SPEAK OUT • BE HEARD• BE CREATIVE •
GO FOR YOUR DREAMS!
Discover how you can:

- handle grouchy, just plain ornery adults

- pass notes in class without getting caught

- avoid life's most embarrassing moments

✳ Scholastic & Book of the Month Club Selection ✳

Girls Know Best celebrates girls' unique voices and wisdom. 38 girls, ages 7-15, share their advice and activities. Everything you need to know ... from the people who've been there: girls just like you!

160 pages, black and white collage art, $8.95 softcover

LISTEN UP!
GIRLS HAVE MORE TO SAY!
More girl wisdom on:

- how to have the best slumber party ever

- discovering the meanings of your dreams

- overcoming any obstacle, whenever, wherever

160 pages, black and white collage art, $8.95 softcover

GIRLS CANNOT BE SILENCED!
EVEN MORE GIRL TALK!
Answers all your questions about:

- different religions

- starting your own rock band

- whether alternative schooling is for you and, of course, much, much more!

132 pages, black and white collage art, $8.95 softcover

YOU GO GIRL!

Learn how to master your:

- Body: feeding and training your incredible machine

- Mind: talking yourself into sports success

- Spirit: dealing with others' negativity

Throw Like a Girl gives you information and inspiration to get involved in sports: for fun, for fitness, and even for a career. Hear from the experts, the stars, and from girls like you. Learn about sports nutrition and exercises while you're picking up tips for dealing with pushy coaches, teammates, and, oh yes, even parents.

160 pages, black and white collage art, $10.95 softcover

GROWING UP JUST GOT A LITTLE EASIER

Life can be tough, especially when you're in between everything. *The Girls' Life Guide to Growing Up* helps relieve the stress of "tweendom" and "teendom" and shows you how to deal with:

- She's All That—Or is She? The myths of hangin' with the "in" crowd are busted by girls who have been there.

- What Kind of Smart Are You? Intelligence is more than a grade on a math test. This quiz reveals your true talents.

- Whose Body Is This, Anyway? Yeah, you're going through some crazy changes. Know what to expect and how to cope.

✷ Scholastic Book Club Selection ✷

It's as cool an advice book as you'll ever want, written by the staff of your favorite magazine, *Girls Life*. Take the quizzes, read the chapters and become self aware! See what guys really think about all this girl stuff, and laugh out loud as you read about everything from friends, family, crushes, school, your body, and most of all, you!

272 pages, black and white illustrations, $11.95 softcover

TO ORDER ANY OF THE BOOKS LISTED HERE OR TO REQUEST A CATALOG, PLEASE CONTACT US OR MAIL US THIS ORDER FORM.

Name_____

Address_____

City _____ State/Province _____ Zip/Postal Code _____

Country _____

Phone Number_____

Title Quantity   Price   Total

_____

_____

_____

_____

_____

_____

                                        Subtotal _____

                          Shipping (see below) _____

                                        Total _____

We accept Visa, MasterCard, and American Express, or send a check or money order payable to Beyond Words Publishing.

Credit Card Number _____ Exp. Date_____

Shipping Rates (within the United States only)
First book: $3.00   Each additional book: $1.00
Please call for special shipping services (overnight or international).

Beyond Words Publishing, Inc.
20827 NW Cornell Road, Suite 500
Hillsboro, OR 97124-9808

Or contact us by phone: 1-800-284-9673
In Oregon (503) 531-8700
fax: (503) 531-8773
email: *sales@beyondword.com*